The Complete
SALUKI

DIANA AND KEN ALLAN

HOWELL
BOOK HOUSE

New York

Maxwell Macmillan Canada
Toronto

Maxwell Macmillan International
New York Oxford Singapore Sydney

Howell Book House
Macmillan Publishing Company
866 Third Avenue
New York, NY 10022

Maxwell Macmillan Canada, Inc.
1200 Eglinton Avenue East, Suite 200
Don Mills, Ontario M3C 3N1

0-87605-274-X
Library of Congress-in-Publication Data

Allan, Diana.
     The complete Saluki / Diana and Ken Allan.
         p. cm.
      ISBN 0-87605-274-X
      1. Saluki. I. Allan, Ken. II. Title.
    SF429.S33A44 1991
    636.7'53—dc20   91-9227   CIP

Maxwell Macmillan is part of the Maxwell Communication Group of Companies.

Macmillan books are available at special discounts for bulk purchases for sales promotions, premiums, fund-raising, or educational use. For details, contact:

Special Sales Director
Macmillan Publishing Company
866 Third Avenue
New York, NY 10022

10 9 8 7 6 5 4 3 2 1

Printed in Singapore

**To Abi, who captivated our hearts and taught us
the ways of the Saluki – her memory will never fade.**

ACKNOWLEDGEMENTS

We are deeply indebted to the many friends who have participated in the compilation of *The Complete Saluki* and in particular to Mrs Christina Ormsby, who gave her time and expertise so readily, without her help our task would have been a lot more difficult. Chris was responsible for checking our contents for correctness and authenticity, a daunting task, but one which was carried out to perfection. To Chris we give our sincere thanks.

Our friend Susan Schroder, from California, who helped us enormously with the American section, she spent many hours on the telephone and at the typewriter sifting through and sorting out all the necessary information for us. Thank you Susan, a true friend indeed.

Our grateful thanks go also to Hope and David Waters for allowing us to quote from their magnificent book *The Saluki In History, Art And Sport*

We are also indebted to Marion Alexander and Vicky Clarke for their help on the American Open Field Coursing section, and Jack and Ruth Southam for furnishing us with all the necessary information regarding lure coursing. Our sincere thanks to all of you.

Last, but definitely not least, our sincere gratitude to everyone who so readily sent photographs and supplied information, usually at short notice. Without your contributions this book would be incomplete.

Preface

Like dream-creatures!
Their footfalls
Do not strum the grass
Nor disorder it;

Walking,
It is not daintiness
But delicacy
That produces no echo;

Running,
Fleet-footed
They look not to right nor left,
Choosing the intuitive way,
For they are noble;

Leaping,
They appear to fly!
Feathered limbs
Clean as the wings of angels;

At rest,
Their almond eyes
Reflect no sadness,
Simply an adoration
Of what is:

A contemplation of faith.
They accept morsels of food
With gentleness,
Fastidious,
Ungreedy.

Gifts from God
They are called by their earliest
                    companions
Who did not sell them
But placed them with friends
As tributes to friendship
And as homage!

They are dogs, said a wise man,
they are Salukis

A. L. Hendriks

Reproduced by kind permission of *The Saluki*

Contents

Kurdish Hounds, circa 1860.

Chapter One

THE DESERT HOUND

The true origin of this beautiful breed of Arabian hunting hound is lost in the mists of time and the shifting sands of the desert; even the source of the name 'Saluki' is a mystery. Saluki is an anglicism of the Arabic word salūqī, and research through medieval literature, written in Arabic, reveals several places which may have given their name to the hound of the desert. Some lexicographers have suggested that the origin of the word was derived from a town called Saluk, in Southern Arabia, which no longer exists. Saluk or Salūq was famous for its armour and hounds, and reference to the hounds is made in an early Arab verse: "Oh my hound brought by Kings from Saluk". Another line from a verse composed by an Umayyad poet reads: "They have with them their hounds of Salūq, like horses wheeling in battle, dragging on their halters." There is another place named Salūq in Armenia, to the west of the Caspian Sea. Other Arabic sources mention two towns with the name Salūqiyah, from which the saluqi might have been derived. The last and perhaps the most plausible suggestion is that the name saluqi could be derived from Seleucia (Salūqiyah in Arabic), a city on the west bank of the Tigris south of Baghdad, founded by Seleucus I in 312BC. The city was the capital of the Seleucid dynasty which survived down to circa 65AD. This implies that the word Saluki does not

A Persian Greyhound, by Harrison Weir. 19th Century.

Levrier Persian 'Mesjed' from Les Races des Chiens, 1905.

originate from one specific place, but is associated with the vast Middle Eastern Empire of the Seleucid dynasty.

Another interesting point that derives from investigating the origin of the name Saluki, is that both the words Saluki and Sloughi are corruptions of the Arabic Saluqi, the former English and the latter French. Although both are registered as separate breeds by the governing bodies of the dog world, and now have different Breed Standards, it is almost certain that at one time they were the same single basic type of gazehound.

The Saluki is also referred to as Slughi, Shami and Tazi. The Honourable Florence Amherst, the first President of the Saluki or Gazelle Hound Club, used the word Slughi to describe all the varieties of Salukis, Shami for all feathered types, and Tazi, which means literally "Arabian", for the Persian hound. It should be emphasised that we are discussing the possible source of the name of the hound in Arab tradition, not the origin of the hound itself.

Tracing the beginnings of the Saluki as a breed is like assembling a giant jigsaw puzzle with many of the important parts missing. Perhaps we will never discover the true origin and development of this historic hound. However, studying the antiquity of these beautiful hounds reveals that they have hunted for the ancient Egyptians and for their Mesopotamian masters, and they were accomplished providers of food for the nomadic Arab tribes who roamed the desert lands of the Arabian Peninsula. The Saluki was also found in Syria, the Valleys of the Euphrates and Tigris, Kurdistan, Persia, Turkestan, Sinai Peninsula, Abyssinia and Northern Africa.

One of the earliest recorded illustrations of sighthounds is a stamp seal found at Tepe Gawra, near Nineveh (Assyria), dated 2000 to 3000BC. Charles Bache, a member of the excavation team, commented on the find in 1936: "Saluki, in various poses, proving that the breed is an exceedingly old one. Also the very fact that the Saluki is depicted on seals shows the high esteem in which this graceful and useful dog was held." Salukis are also depicted throughout the early Egyptian civilisation: a fresco at Western Thebes, circa 1400BC, shows the Great Governor Rekh-ma-ra receiving a procession of tributes from conquered lands, among which are three Salukis, a golden, red, and a white. On the wall of Nebamun's tomb about 1490BC, a parti-coloured Saluki is depicted, wearing a broad collar. Excavations from Tutankhamen's tomb disclosed other examples of Salukis, including scenes on a wooden funerary casket. One side depicts Tutankhamen riding into battle in a chariot accompanied by two white Salukis. On the other side a similar scene shows Salukis assisting in the defeat of the Pharaoh's African foes. The lid of the casket displays two other scenes of Salukis hunting a gazelle and attacking a lion.

It is easy to enthuse about this graceful hound of such aesthetic elegance, and to

Persian miniature, Tapkapi Museum.

Two Salukis, the lower one with cropped ears, circa 14th century.

romance, or dream, about its place in early civilisations, but unfortunately it can only be conjecture. However, the hound that graces our show ring today has been predominately inherited from the nomadic Bedouin, and fortunately its place within that society has been well documented in Arabian writings and by explorers of the Arabian culture. The Saluki's speed, endurance and beauty have become legendary. Poets have written in praise of their achievements; artists, and latterly photographers, have captured their prowess on canvas and film.

The Bedouin lived in tribal groups in the harsh environment of the desert, and the Saluki provided both sport and food for their masters. The Bedouin led a nomadic life, moving constantly to seek fresh grazing ground and water holes for their herds of camels, goats, sheep and horses. Each tribe moved within certain geographical limitations of migration, following a pattern of life that changed little over the years. Salukis, as well as hawks and falcons were kept for hunting and sport, often working together in the chase. Contrasting types of Salukis also existed within the different tribes and geographic areas of the continent, and both feathered and smooth Salukis existed side by side. Sometimes the ears of the feathered types were cropped to prevent the feathering becoming caught up in the scrub. Each tribe specialised in keeping its breeding pure and maintaining an efficient hunting strain of hound. Whether smooth or feathered, the Saluki was bred to fulfill its role within the nomadic society. Its appearance was of grace, symmetry, strength and speed, combined with endurance and gentleness; it displayed a proud head carriage, a long arched neck, a curved tail, which it used as a rudder to steer itself over the windswept desert, and it had exceptionally keen eyes. In disposition the Saluki is extremely faithful and devoted to its master and is dependent on human affection. This is a breed that cannot bear rough treatment, but can be taught and trained with gentleness, firmness and patience, and can be almost human in its understanding.

H. R. P. Dickson states that the Bedouin only pay attention to the following:

a) The snout or muzzle must be long and narrow – this for breed.
b) The girth at chest must be deep, the deeper the better – this for staying power.
c) The girth at waist must be fine – this is for speed.
d) The hocks must be well let down – this also for speed.
e) The width between the tops of the thigh bones measured on the back must be good, i.e. at least the width of the hand including the thumb – this for speed.

Great care was exercised to keep the breeding of the Saluki pure. Pedigrees were learnt by heart and transferred from generation to generation by word of mouth. Breeding was exercised carefully, and few can doubt the skill of Arab breeding – the

Arab-bred horses are sufficient testimony. In fact, the similarity between the Saluki and the horse is a recurring theme throughout Arab literature. One example illustrates this: "Amr asked a cousin of his in Syria to buy a horse for him. The cousin replied, "I have no knowledge of horses." Muslim said, "Are you not a hunting man?" "Yes." "Then look for everything which you consider good in the hound and seek it in the horse." His cousin bought him a horse the like of which was not found among the Bedouin Arabs.

The importance of the Saluki to each family and tribal unit as a meat-provider cannot be over-emphasised. The Saluki enjoyed a far superior position to that of ordinary dogs (kelbs) who were considered unclean and used as guard dogs. Muslim religion regards all dogs as unclean and therefore they are not permitted into the tents. The Saluki, however, was not considered a dog but a Saluki, El Hor 'the noble one', and therefore held a position of esteem within the Arab household. The hounds were permitted to wander freely within the tent, to eat the same food as their masters, mainly rice, meat (when available) and dates, and even to sleep in the women's quarters. Paradoxically, Muslims are prohibited from eating game that is not slaughtered in the prescribed manner. The problem regarding game caught by a Saluki was resolved by the Prophet declaring that so long as the hunter pronounced the basmalah when the hounds were released after the quarry, and providing the game was caught by the hunter's own hounds and they had made no attempt to eat or mutilate the game, it was lawful to eat it. This pronouncement assured the future of hunting in Islam and cemented the privileged status of the Saluki in Arab life.

Salukis were so highly valued by the Bedouin that they were never sold; sometimes one was presented as a gift to a friend or distinguished guest as a mark of friendship or respect. Individual families within each tribe probably kept about two hounds to provide food. Great care was taken to prevent unwanted pregnancies or accidental mating with the guard dogs. One method used to avoid mating was to tie the hind leg of the bitch to her collar, so that the only comfortable position she could achieve was to lie down. A bitch in whelp was looked after by the women and children within the family. When the bitch was ready to whelp, the women or servants dug a slanting pit in the sand, three to four feet deep, and covered it over with sticks and brushwood, laying a layer of earth over the top. An entrance to the inclined way was left for the expectant mother, so that she could have her young in a cool and comfortable place.

The Saluki was kept primarily for hunting hare and gazelle (now a protected species); the oryx was also a quarry and Salukis were not adverse to catching the odd Houbara. Hare hunting was usually carried out by huntsmen beating out stretches of ground to raise the hare, then two or three Salukis would chase and kill the quarry. Sometimes the Saluki was carried on the back of a horse or camel to keep it fresh for the hunt. An extract from Major Cheesman's book *In Unknown Arabia* gives an exciting account of a Saluki coursing the hare: "An hour later, another hare was moved a long way ahead, and by the time the Saluki was pushed off the camel she must have started with a lead of 400 yards. It was a splendid sight to see him really extended and overhauling her with long strides on the broad plain. The hare was quite out of sight when he first turned her; we could only follow the hunt by the movements of the dog, who seemed to be tiring with the length of the first spurt, and we imagined the hare was going to outrun him in the open. At the second turn the pair were nearer, and we saw him turn and try to grab her, and the third time he had her. Having killed her, he looked around and found we were too far out of the picture to count; so picking up his prize, he carried it to a suitable bush surrounded by sand, where he proceeded to dig a hole and give her a decent burial. When at last we got the lumbering camels on the scene, she was completely hidden in sand and the Saluki recovering his breath in another quarter." In another extract from the same publication is a description of how the Saluki keeps cool between hunts: "Another trick for keeping cool practised by the dog during our half-hour halts, was to select the shade of the thickest bush and scratch off the top layer; then squatting down in quite a human attitude, with his hind legs sticking out in front, he would throw up the sand against his body until he was half buried in the cool sand."

The principal hunting prize, however, was the gazelle, which was coursed by the Saluki, usually in conjunction with the hawk. The combination of a falcon hunting with Salukis was a popular sport developed over the centuries. The person who is going to fly the hawk rides with it on his wrist, with the rest of the hunting party following. When a herd of gazelle is sighted, the hawk is set loose and the hounds are released. The Salukis follow the hawk until the quarry is sighted, then both hawk and Salukis will pursue one individual gazelle as a target, the hawk eventually swooping down on to the quarry and the Salukis grasping and holding the gazelle until the riders arrive on the scene. The gazelle is as swift, perhaps even faster, than the Saluki, but the Saluki possesses superior stamina. J. Wentworth Day in his book *The Dog in Sport* recounts a gazelle hunt:

"...Abruptly the sheik turned his head, sudden excitement on his face, beckoned us forward, and with a plunge was over the rise, galloping madly. My stallion sprang forward. There was no question of trot or canter. It was a full gallop. The sheik was a hundred yards in front, his robes billowing. Ahead of him, flying across the desert, was the sudden spectacle of a full-grown gazelle buck, travelling like the wind, the two Salukis hard on his heels. I sat down to ride. It was an armchair ride. No English hunter, no park hack, was ever so comfortable as the Arab horse on his native desert.

Saluki in the Desert.   Sir T. J. Clark.

Hounds in the Desert of North Africa.

I believed now the words of Shafi, my shikari, who had said the night before, comforting me, 'Sheik's horse all good. That horse rides like silk.' He rode indeed like silk. The wind whipped my face. Sharp and cool it came from Libya, from far Cyrenaica, from Tripoli beyond, from all the hills and deserts that lay between my horse's wide nostrils and the far Atlantic beaches. This was riding. An English gallop, even a hunting run, seemed a patchwork affair, a back garden compromise. On and on, the sharp, soft beat of hoofs thudding on the desert, the lithe, tireless energy beneath one, the smooth flowing action – here was a gallop to dream of. Gazelle and hounds disappeared over a rise. We came to the top to see beneath us a sudden yawning slope, cut sheer away, dropping at an angle of thirty degrees. I thought suddenly, fantastically, of those pictures one sees of Italian cavalrymen sliding, stiff-backed on their horses down cliff-faces steep as housesides. We did it. The stallion took charge – more or less. And at the bottom the gazelle jinked suddenly to one side, gliding like a shadow up a narrow wadi that doubled back almost on our track. The hounds overshot him, wheeled, pulled up suddenly in a flying storm of sand, and came racing back on his tracks. But they had lost a good fifty yards. One knew that they knew that they had made fools of themselves. The beat of hoofs echoed back from the wadi walls like muted drum-beats. The gazelle was now a hundred yards ahead, going like the wind. Arabs tell you that they travel at from forty-two to forty-five miles an hour. I can believe every mile of it. And those who have timed them from motor-cars confirm it. Suddenly there was a whoop ahead. Down the wadi-side came tearing the two hounds we had left behind, their Arab footman standing on the rise against the skyline, his galabia blown out like a banner. The buck jinked again. He jinked twice. But it was near the end. The two fresh hounds, turning like taxis, almost in their own length, doubled and gained on him. Again he jinked, and the leading hound took him in the shoulder like a torpedo, bowled him over like a rabbit. Horsemen and hounds arrived in a clutter. The sheik was off his mount in a flash, whipped out a thin knife, plunged it into the buck's throat. That was my first gazelle hunt with the hunting dogs of the desert."

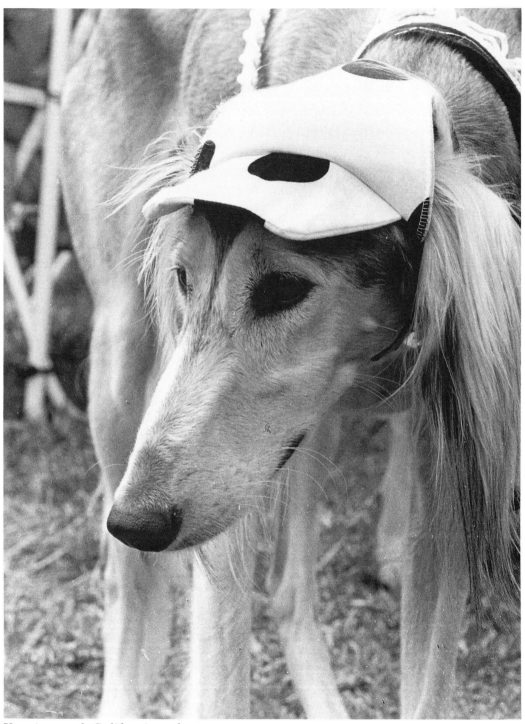

Keeping cool, California style.

Chapter Two

THE SHOW SALUKI
IN AMERICA

There is little documented evidence regarding the introduction of the Saluki into America. 1927 saw the inauguration of the Saluki Club of America and recognition of the Saluki by the American Kennel Club. The first recorded Saluki in America was in 1861, when Colonel H.N. Fisher of Boston imported a Saluki from Thebes. Breeding of Salukis, based on Sarona and Grevel lines was started during the mid-1920s. The first Saluki Champions listed by the American Kennel Club were recorded in 1931: Sarona Dhole (Sarona Kelb ex Sarona Nurnisha), Sand Spring Sheba (Ch. Sheik of Ro Akbar ex Zillah of Sarona) and Malikah Al Bararey Jibal (Ch. Sheik of Ro Akbar ex Zillah of Sarona). In 1932, Mr Edward K. Aldrich Jnr, in Rhode Island, bought two Amherstia bitches and a dog, bred from Sarona imports, to start his Diamond Hill kennels. Mr Aldrich Jnr bred, among other Champions, Am. Ch. Marjan II who became the foundation sire of Mrs Anna Marie Paterno's El Retiro kennels, and Am. Ch. Valda, who started Mrs Esther Knapp's Pine Paddocks kennels. Am. Ch. Marjan II was to become the first Saluki in America to win Best in

The breed rings, Westminster Kennel Club, Madison Square Garden, New York.

Show; he also won the Hound Group at Westminster. Another notable Saluki to come out of the Diamond Hill kennels was Ch. Kataf (Akbar Malik ex Ch. Valda), who won a total of twenty-six Groups.

Another early pioneer of the breed was Mrs Marjorie Kemm of the Anfa kennels, who bred Ch. Anfa's Nukhaila Farouk (Ch. Abdul Farouk 11 of Pine Paddocks ex El Retiro's Aida), known as 'Freckles'. One of her progeny, Ch. Anfa's Sarona ('Aggie') sired by Anfa's Zahir-U-Din, was also shown in Europe and became the first American-bred to earn the international CACIB title. 'Freckles' was a granddaughter of the late King Ibn Saud of Arabia's hunting hound, Ch. Abdul Farouk. Farouk had been presented, together with a suitable mate, to an English Field Marshall while he was a guest of the king during the war. After the war, the Field Marshall moved to Washington D.C. to head the British Joint Chiefs of Staff. City life did not suit the two desert hounds and they eventually joined Mrs Knapp at her kennels. The honour of becoming the first smooth Saluki Champion fell to Mrs Knapp's dog Rasim Ramullah of Pine Paddocks in 1948. Pine Paddocks also held the BIS record for Salukis for many years. The American fancy owes a great deal to these early breeders who battled through difficult times to maintain numbers, keeping the Saluki eligible for AKC registration. Between 1931 and 1947 thirty-six Salukis are listed as gaining their titles in the American Saluki Association's

Int. Am. Can. Mex. Venz. Ch. Bel S'mbran Aba Fantasia (Int. Ch. Bel S'mbran Bachrach CC CM FCH ex Bayt Shahin Ana a Bel S'mbran), owned and bred by George and Sally Bell.

Linda Lindt.

Int. Am. Can. Mex. Ch. Bel S'mbran Promise of Atallah FCH (Ch. Springtime Euphrates Jaadan ex Ch. Bel S'mbran Aba Fantasia), owned and bred by George and Sally Bell.

Krystl, showing a good front, under International judge Terry Thorn at Channel City Kennel Club, Santa Barbara, 1988.

Ch. Jatara's Irish Krystl (Ch. Sundown Darjalan ex Ch. Bejon Sasha of Jatara). Bred and owned by Jackie Harrington.

Caravanserai of American Kennel Club Champions. By comparison, in the latest published edition, one hundred and seventy Champions are listed in the last recorded entry – proof of the Saluki's rise in popularity.

On the East Coast, Miss N. Peters started her Warm Valley kennels from stock descending from the Diamond Hill strain. One of her most influential dogs was Warm Valley's Beloved Infidel, a daughter of Mrs Knapp's Ch. Abdul Faruuk II of Pine Paddocks. Two of the most notable descendants of Infidel were Miss Mimi Carlyle's Ch. Canem-Dei's Kitan Tiy Taj, and Ch. Canem-Dei's El Salta 'Aun. Ch. Canem-Dei's Kitan Tiy Taj (Ch. Warm Valley's Tiyson ex Ch. Kitan Aiyila of Canem-Dei), a Canadian and American Champion, won two Best in Shows, nine Hound Groups and eighty-nine Best of Breeds. Taj was the first Saluki bitch to win a Best in Show and produced seven Champion offspring before her untimely death at seven years of age. Ch. Canem-Deis El Salta 'Aun (Warm Valley's Tiygre ex Ch. Kitan Aiyila of Canem-Dei) gained both American and Canadian titles and his Field title. He surpassed all existing records within the breed, winning thirteen Best in Shows, fifty Hound Groups and one hundred and fifty-one Best of Breeds. He was the second Saluki in history to win the Hound Group at Westminster, New York in 1976, and was in the Top Ten Hounds in America for three years, and a Top Ten Sighthound for four years.

On the West Coast Wayne and Marlys Jensen's influential Jen Araby kennel started in the early forties. Their line originated from Diamond Hill, Pine Paddocks and English stock. Numerous Champions have emanated from this kennel and provided foundation stock for many other breeders. Judith Myers, writing in the *Saluki World,* discusses the Jen Araby kennel: "As a breeder Wayne Jensen needs no introduction to American fanciers. Folk less conversant with American dogs can rest assured that the Jen Araby dogs are based on years of devotion and years of successful and improving breeding. Among many things we have admired in the practise of this breeder is his technique of importing, which balanced an astute knowledge of the lines and specific dogs behind each import, and this was never based on the mere fact of a line being in the winner's circle. Imports were selected, not merely for pedigree alone, and in this respect the Jen Araby programme could well be studied by any novice breeder as an example of astuteness, planning and directly related thought. As a man who obviously prefers to rely on results rather than promises (how many ads have you ever seen that have originated from Wayne Jensen?), Wayne Jensen is to be congratulated. After all is said and done – the proof of the pudding lies in his achievement for the breed." Ch. Jen Araby Jurwadi Bey, an outcross sired by the English import Knightellington Djado out of Ch. Jen Araby Berkitaten, became the first Saluki to be awarded three Best of Breeds at the

Wayne and Marlys Jensen's Jen Araby Kanti winning BOB and Winners Dog, Lompoc Valley Kennel Club, under judge Frank Sabella.

prestigious Santa Barbara Show (George and Sally Bell's Ch. Bel S'mbran Promise of Atallah FCH equalled this achievement in 1983, 1984 and 1985), and gained eighty Best of Breeds during his show career. He also has thirty Champion offspring to his credit. Jurwadi Bey was a rich red-grizzle saddled with mahogany brown-black. Bo Bengston wrote in his 1979 Santa Barbara critique: "He is almost impossible to fault structurally and his expression literally sent shivers down my spine... His movement is incredible for his age and perfectly true, both coming and going; beautiful fringe and furnishings. Possibly the only Saluki I have seen which combines complete soundness and complete elegance. An unforgettable dog."

'Kitten', Ch. Jen Araby Mumtaz Mahal (Ch. Jen Araby Diamond Jim ex Ch. Jen Araby Feydaan), was another outstanding Saluki to emerge from the Jen Araby kennel. Gary Roush of *The Saluki Quarterly* wrote the following: "She has a uniqueness of style, grace, presence and symmetry that never failed her. She probably wasn't perfect, as perhaps no Saluki is, but in her presence you thought so."

The Srinagar kennel was founded on the West Coast by Dr Winafred and Miss Afton Lucas during the sixties. They used Jen Araby and English Daxlore lines, and have had a profound influence on the breed with their very active breeding programme.Ch. Sringar Mahina Anumati (Am. Can. Ch. Sringar Jen Araby Krsina ex Ch. Sringar Jen Araby Teja CC) was one of Afton Lucas's all time favourites and her constant companion. Anumati had elegance and grace coupled with soundness. She won her first major at nine months and her second at Westminster KC in 1968. Her next win was another major and she completed her Championship with Winners Bitch and Best of Winners at the Saluki Club of America Specialty Show. As a brood bitch she produced, among others, Ch. Sringar Arya Vihara. Vihara was sired by Ch. Sringar Zanande Sayf Samira (who was later transferred to Australia where he set new records within the breed). Vihara inherited from his parents a balanced conformation and a flowing movement; he achieved his Championship title at eighteen months of age.

As in Britain, the Saluki has become more popular in recent years, and many more breeders are appearing on the scene. Entries at the major Specialty Shows run by Saluki clubs are large, with the Saluki Club of America's Specialty (SCOA) held in Lexington, Kentucky attracting entries approaching five hundred Salukis. The SOCA Specialty is held in conjunction with The Egyptian Event (held by Arab horse breeders), it is held over four days and is a veritable festival for the Saluki. Judging is carried out during all of the days; starting with the Sweepstakes on day one, and breed judging over the remaining three days. In 1990 over eighty dogs competed in the Best of Breed class – certainly the biggest entry we have ever seen. Other events include Obedience Trials, Lure Coursing and a fancy dress parade where both handlers and Salukis are dressed for the occasion. If all that is not enough, you can attend Saluki lectures, buy from an enormous range of Saluki-goods, participate in auctions, and of course, meet many old friends to exchange views and opinions. In the early sixties a small group of Californian Saluki enthusiasts struggled to form a club "dedicated to the fulfilment of the many faceted potentials of the Saluki." Saluki people from outside the state wished to join this fledgling organisation and soon the California Saluki Fanciers became the Western Saluki Association, which in turn, quickly evolved into the American Saluki Association. Today it boasts an international membership. The ASA produces a quarterly magazine for its members, the *ASA Newsletter,* and it worth joining the club to receive this superb publication. In 1963 the ASA commenced support of the Saluki classes at Santa Barbara and started a glorious tradition in the Saluki show circuit. The Santa Barbara Show is a must for every Saluki enthusiast. In 1988 the ASA celebrated its twenty-fifth anniversary at the Santa Barbara Kennel Club, and almost two hundred Salukis attended. Mrs Hope Waters had the honour of judging the bitch classes, with her husband Lt. Cmdr David Waters officiating the dogs. In the evening a superb exhibition was staged with many magnificent exhibits of Saluki related sighthound art on display. The Santa Barbara experience is summed up by Karen Black (Sundown): "We do not come to Santa Barbara to win. We come to celebrate the Saluki."

The prestigious Westminster Kennel Club Show, held in February each year at the Madison Square Gardens, New York is another show that is well worth a visit by any serious dog fancier. Unfortunately, from a Saluki point of view, entries are on the small side. This is because the total show entry is restricted to 25,000 dogs; entries being on a first-received basis. Breed judging is carried out in seven rings throughout the two days of the show, and in the evening the rings are broken up to form one large ring for Group judging. Thousands of spectators sit in tiered seating to cheer on their favourites in the contest for Group Winner and eventual Best in Show. Several Salukis have had success in the Hound Group, but to date, Westminster still awaits its first Saluki Best in Show.

George and Sally Bell have had considerable success in the show ring. Three of their Salukis – Ch. Bel S'mbran Bachrach, Ch. Bel S'mbran Aba Fantasia, and Ch. Bel S'mbran Promise of Atallah – have achieved remarkable wins. Bachrach (Ch. Springtime Euphrates Jaadan ex Am. Can. Ch. Bayt Shahin Vada a Bel S'mbran CC CM) gained International, American Mexican and Venezuelan titles, together with Coursing Champion, Courser of Merit and Field Champion. He was the number one Saluki in 1977, 1978 and 1979, the first sighthound to become both NOFCA Coursing Champion and ASA Lure Coursing Champion, and sired five Best in Show

Salukis. The most commanding of this trio is probably Fantasia, bred from Bachrach to Bayt Shahin Ana a Bel S'mbran. Her impressive record includes: International, American, Canadian, Mexican and Venezuelan show titles, number one Saluki in 1980 and 1981, Hound Group winner at Westminster in 1982, winning twenty BIS awards, and the only Saluki to be simultaneously the number one Saluki in both Canada and the United States. Fantasia returned to Westminster in 1991 to participate in a parade of previous Best in Show or Group Winners. This parade was first held at the one hundredth anniversary and repeated in 1981 and 1986, and is scheduled to be held on a five-yearly cycle. Fantasia represented the breed with typical Saluki aplomb; she still looked most elegant and beautiful, at almost fourteen years of age. Ch. Bel S'mbran Promise of Atallah FC (Ch. Springtime Euphrates ex Ch. Bel S'mbran Aba Fantasia) gained International, American, Canadian and Mexican titles, the number one Saluki in 1985, and won three Best of Breeds at Santa Barbara (equalling Jurwadi Bey's record). Atallah, known as "Twix" was used in the American Kennel Club's Official Breed Standard video to illustrate Saluki movement. He has the correct, lifting side movement and sound rear and front action. Head studies of the dog were also used at a breed seminar conducted by the Saluki Club of America, as an example of the perfect parallel planes that is desirable in a Saluki head. Currently, the top winning Saluki in America is Jackie Harrington's owner-bred Ch. Jatara's Irish Krystl (Ch. Sundown Darjalan ex Ch. Bejon Sasha of Jatara). Krystl has been the Top Winning Saluki for the last three years and has won twenty-one All Breed Best in Shows and ten Specialty Best of Breeds, to date.

When calculating Top Winning Salukis, two different pointing systems are used in the Conformation Rankings. System one credits each best of Breed Winner with a point for each Saluki defeated by virtue of the win. System two credits one point for each dog defeated (of any breed) by virtue of Best of Breed, Group or Best in Show wins. Anyone who is not familiar with the American system may find this very confusing, however, it is quite easy to understand. For example: if your Saluki wins Best of Breed and defeats 100 dogs, it receives 100 points. If this is an All Breed Show and your Saluki goes on to win the Hound Group, it will add to its tally all the points from the other BOB winners in the Group. If your Saluki then wins Best in Show, the final points accumulated will be the sum of all the BOB winners in every Group. Both conformation and ranking tables are regularly published and run annually from the first show held in the calendar year. In order to have a dog that appears within the top ten placements it must be an excellent specimen of the breed, and it needs an awful lot of time and dedication – especially when you consider the distances that exhibitors have to travel in order to compete.

Chapter Three

THE SHOW SALUKI
IN BRITAIN

There is little evidence of Salukis in Britain prior to the end of the nineteenth century. The Crusaders were reputed to have hunted with them in Palestine and brought them back from the Crusades as proof of their pilgrimage. A link with the Crusading period still lingers in the desert with the Arabic name for the feathered variety, "reishan", so called after King Richard Coeur de Lion, who was said to have owned some of these beautiful desert hounds. We do, however, know that a black and tan Persian Greyhound bitch, was bred in the Zoological Gardens, Regent's Park, in 1835 and subsequently exhibited there. A note on the back of an old print showing a Saluki confirms this, and reveals that the dog illustrated was named Zillah and that she was the only specimen of the breed in England at that time. The hound displays similar characteristics to those found in the show ring today, although the face, as depicted, is too pointed and lacks a strong underjaw. The Kennel Club records reveal that the first recorded win for a Saluki at a dog show was in 1875, when a light fawn bitch named Tierma, owned by Mr H. Allan of London, took the honours. The breed started to become established in 1897, when a pair of golden puppies of under ten months (one dog and one bitch), given to the Hon. Florence Amherst by Colonel Jennings Bramley, were imported. The dog, "La'aman" (meaning flash of light), and the bitch, "Ayesha" (after the second wife of Mahomet), had been obtained from the Bedouin tribe of Tahawi in Lower Egypt. These dogs became the foundation of Miss Amherst's kennel, the Amherstias. The Hon. Florence Amherst had been attracted to the breed while working with her father exploring Egyptian tombs and antiquities. Once her interest was aroused, she made a careful study of the breed in its various desert locations and wrote extensively on the Saluki, its environment and characteristics. Historians of the breed will find some confusion regarding the naming of "La'aman". Different writers refer to the first dog owned by Miss Amherst as "LaMaun," "Luma," and "Luman": all are undoubtedly the same animal. He died of old age and his body was presented to the Natural History Museum, London for display and was later transferred to the Tring Museum in Hertfordshire.

Miss Amherst continued to import other Salukis of desert breeding from different geographical regions, and she became a prolific breeder of Salukis, registering 199 puppies from 50 litters, between 1897 to 1937, with the Kennel Club. Her first Champion, and the third recorded within the breed, was Ch. Zobeid, a gold dog bred by Mrs A. Vereker Cowley, winning four Challenge Certificates and gaining his title in 1925. She was later to write: "After careful study of the breed I realised that I was the custodian of a great heritage for the dog world in this country. For that reason, I was most careful not to let the breed pass into other hands without great caution until the exceptional worth of this pure and highly bred race, which has been kept true to type from time immemorial, was understood, for fear that for want of sufficient knowledge of the breed the identity and purity of the race might be lost."

Since there were no classes for Salukis, in the early years Miss Amherst mainly campaigned her hounds in the Foreign Dog Classes, winning at Crufts in 1913 and 1914 with her dog Sultan. Although much curiosity was aroused by the arrival of the Saluki in Britain, they failed to attract exhibitors in any numbers. They started to become more firmly established at the end of the First World War, mostly because officers on military service in the Middle East had been given Salukis by their Bedouin hosts as gifts. The officers had also been invited to desert hunting parties and witnessed the sporting qualities of the Saluki and falcon working together, chasing the gazelle and other quarry.

The most notable of these post-war imports was Ch. Sarona Kelb. Kelb, a black-and-tan dog, was born in Damascus in 1919. He was owned and bred by Brigadier General Lance (Saronas) from two Salukis he had been given. The sire was a white-

Persian Greyhound, "Zillah."

The legendary Ch. Sarona Kelb (Seleughi ex Baalbek), born in June 1919, sire of five Champion sons and five Champion daughters.

black-and-tan dog called Selughi, presented to General Lance by a Syrian Sheikh as a token of friendship, and he was reputedly a very fast and clever coursing dog. The dam, Baalbek, was a small grizzle bitch, given to General Lance by the Kaimarkan of Baalbek. Baalbek had two litters sired by Selughi, and all the resultant progeny were black-and-tans. Ch. Sarona Kelb was imported into England in 1921 and was to become a legend within the breed. He became the first Saluki Dog Champion when Challenge Certificates were awarded, and won his final and twelfth Challenge Certificate at Crufts in 1930 at the age of eleven. Kelb put his stamp on the breed from the outset. He set the standard for future generations by siring five sons and five daughters, who became Champions. The Waters, in their book *The Saluki In History, Art And Sport*, state that by mid-1968 the majority of the forty-nine dogs and forty-five bitches that had by then become Champions, were descendants of Kelb. In his book *The New Book Of The Dog*, E. C. Ash quotes General Lance, who describes Kelb as excelling in "...soundness, quality and feather, was a wonderful coursing dog, and had killed gazelle in Palestine." The choice of name, however does pose an interesting question. Why was he named after the generic Arab term for all dogs, who are considered to be unclean? The only explanation we can find appears in an article in *Country Life*, July 25th 1925. "Kelb received his appellation in Damascus during the absence of his master on leave, but of its inappropriateness there can be no doubt. In an informative letter to General Lance, Mr H. L. Powell, who has travelled much in the East, considers that the term Saluki was given to the breed by the Turks, on first obtaining them from the Seljuk tribe, and so we get through Seljuki the corruptions Saluki, Salaak, Saluk or Salag. Among the tribes Salukis are never referred to as kelb or cheeb, the Arabic word for dog. Dining with a sheikh one night off a bustard that had fallen to a Saka falcon and Salukis, Mr Powell, venturing upon the delicate topic of religion, asked him how he could enjoy food that had been defiled by the touch of dogs. The reply was that 'Salukis are not dogs; they are Salukis, and were given to us by Allah for our amusement and benefit.' "

The first meeting of the Saluki or Gazelle Hound Club was held after the Crufts Dogs Show in the Agricultural Hall, Islington, London on February 8th 1923 when fourteen interested Saluki owners met. The declared objective of the club was: "..to promote and encourage the breeding of Salukis, to spread interest in the breed by making its qualities more widely known, and to encourage the exhibition of the breed by obtaining classes for it at suitable Dog Shows, and by giving special prizes." The Hon. Florence Amherst was elected President (a position she held until 1946), Brigadier General F. Lance was Vice-President, Mr L. Crouch was Hon. Treasurer and Mrs Gladys Lance was Secretary. The first elected Committee

The Hon. Florence Amherst's Ch. Zobeid with his brother Farhan.

Saluki Club Members Show, Tattersall's 1926.

members were: Mrs L. Armstrong, Mrs L. Crouch, Miss M. Grey, Major Bayne
Jardine, Miss S. Kerrison, Mrs Foster Mitchell and Lt. A. R. Spurgin. The standard
of points was the main area of discussion, and the meeting closed without reaching a
final agreement. The main disagreement was over the minimum acceptable height to
be allowed. At a meeting held on February 22nd 1923, the Standard of Points and
the Club Rules were drawn up and agreed. The standard adopted was loose enough
to accommodate all types of Saluki from the smallest of the "Amherstias" to the
largest of the "Saronas", and also preserved colour variation and the finer points of
the breed. The Club was officially recognised by the Kennel Club on April 24th
1923. On July 17th 1923 the Saluki became a recognised breed under the Hound
Section of Sporting Dogs, and Challenge Certificates were allocated. At the end of
the first year the membership stood at forty persons – today it numbers some four
hundred members.

Salukis were first classified as a breed at the Kensington Canine Society Show in
April 1923; there were eleven entries out of five classes. Challenge Certificates were
first competed for at the Kennel Club Show at Crystal Palace in October 1923.
Twelve classes were scheduled: seven were allocated for the feathered variety and
five for the smooth variety. Sarona Kelb won the Dog CC and Mrs L. W. Crouch's
Orchard Shahin won the Bitch CC. Modern showgoers will be surprised by the
allocation of classes for the smooth Saluki. In the formative years it was normal to
have both smooth and feathered classifications scheduled, but gradually the smooth
classes were dropped due to lack of support. The first Saluki to obtain the title of
Champion was Orchard Shahin, who won the first three shows at which Challenge
Certificates were contested. Shahin was a black-white-and-tan-parti bitch owned by
Mrs L. W. Crouch, and bred by General Lance out of Sarona Kelb and Sarona
Sarona. She won a total of ten Challenge Certificates. Mrs Crouch's (Orchard)
involvement with Salukis began in 1922 – she had previously owned a renowned
kennel of poodles. Between 1924 and 1938 she registered sixteen Saluki litters with
the Kennel Club and six progeny became Champions. Sadly, the kennels closed with
the outbreak of the Second World War and did not reopen. The line was carried on
through hounds owned by Mrs R. G. Michelmore (Nal). Other early pioneers of the
breed were: Miss Sybil Kerrison (The Iraqs), Mrs Harold Barr (The Grevels), Miss
Doxford (The Ruritanias), and Miss Joan Mitchell (Nablous).

Miss Kerrison, of the Iraqs prefix, was a founder member of the Saluki or Gazelle
Hound Club and elected committee member. She was a coursing enthusiast, and was
elected Honorary Coursing Secretary in 1927. She was responsible for many a good
day's coursing with Salukis in Oxfordshire, where she lived for a number of years.
Miss Kerrison bred four litters which produced three Champions. An article from

Saluki Club Members Show, Tattersall's 1929.

Ch. Nenga of Ruritania 3CCs (Ch. Tarzan of Ruritania ex Sarona Nurnisha). Owner/Breeder: Miss A. Doxford.

Ch. Orchard Ahmud (Orchard Lekim ex Ch. Orchard Mousa), litter brother to Ch. Orchard Mahbubah, in 1935 at two years of age. Owner/Breeder: Mrs L. Crouch.

Our Dogs in 1925, featuring her kennel, stated: "One can never review this stud without feeling that one is turning over a new page in Saluki glamour. The fancy has long been accustomed to accepting as a commonplace the exquisite quality and superlative merit of the Iraq Salukis, and their unassailable position in the van of the breed; but no one has ceased to wonder at their marvellous muscle, their perfect physical fitness, and their mental alertness and unique intelligence. Looking at the Iraq Hounds, one understands why Eastern princes value the breed far above rubies, why Arab chiefs rate them higher than kings' ransoms."

Mrs I. H. Barr (Grevel) was a successful Wolfhound breeder before becoming interested in Salukis. Her first Saluki was an imported smooth bitch called Egyptian Lady, who was mated in 1924. In 1925 her daughter Miss H. I. H. Barr took over the breeding, and the Grevel Salukis became architects of the breed's early eminence, having a large influence in the Saluki's progress and recognition on both sides of the Atlantic. Although none of the Grevel Salukis were to become Champions, their influence appears behind pedigrees in England and abroad. Miss Doxford's (Ruritanias) was a renowned breeder and owner of Deerhounds. Her first Saluki was

Ch. Sara of Shammar (Abdul of Shammar ex Bariza Mazuri of Shammar).
Owner/Breeder: Mrs H. M. Parkhouse.

a cream imported bitch called Tazi of Abbotsford. Tazi was purchased from Mrs L. Armstrong in 1920 and re-registered as Tazi of Ruritania. On June 18th 1923 Tazi produced a litter of twelve puppies, sired by Sarona Kelb. Two of these pups went on to become Champions, Ch. Hassan and Ch. Tarzan of Ruritania; and Mrs Armstrong became the first Saluki breeder to produce two Champions from the same litter. Ch. Hassan, winner of five Challenge Certificates, was an exquisite red dog, beautiful in outline, with a lovely head, graceful neck and profuse in feathering. Ch. Tarzan, winner of three Challenge Certificates, was a captivating aristocratic red dog, very alluring in conformation and very sound. Between 1923 and 1937, Miss Doxford bred twenty-seven litters and owned twelve Champions; seven of whom were home-bred. Miss Joan F. Mitchell (Nablous) joined the Saluki or Gazelle Hound Club in 1924. She had worked in Palestine as matron of a hospital in Nablous, and on her retirement she returned to England bringing two Salukis – littermates Ebni and Binte El Nablous, sired by Jack of Jerusalem, a Saluki well thought of in the area where she had lived. The Nablous Salukis were of the smaller type and were very graceful. The first Saluki or Gazelle Hound Club Members Show was held in beautiful weather at St. John's Lodge, Regent's Park, London on July 6th 1924; it attracted an entry of 111 dogs from 15 exhibitors. In 1925 the Members Show had an entry of 150 dogs in 18 classes. The same year British-bred Salukis were exported to America, Sweden and France. The Saluki was now becoming established worldwide in the show ring. However, the outbreak of World War Two brought breeding almost to a standstill.

In England three notable kennels bridged the Pre/Post-wars; the Shammars, the Knightellingtons and the Mazuris. Mrs Parkhouse's (the Shammars) foundation lines were predominantly Orchard and Sarona. Her second Saluki, Ch. Nal Janzi, bred by Mrs R. Michelmore, won seven Challenge Certificates and was twice Best of Breed at Crufts in 1938 and 1939. In 1941 *Our Dogs* said of him: "In formation, action and temperament he is ambition's dream come true, and everybody is familiar with his magnificent feathering, perfect head, eyes, expression – features which seem well-nigh a commonplace in the Shammar hounds." Ch. Nal Janzi was the last pre-war Champion, and one of his progeny, Ch. Selim of Shammar had the honour of becoming the first post-war Champion. Although Mrs Parkhouse only bred five litters, her breeding had a considerable influence on the breed. In all, she owned six Champions, of which three were home-bred. Mrs Parkhouse was elected President of the Saluki or Gazelle Hound Club in 1964, a position which she held for some twenty years.

Mrs Gwen Angel (the Mazuris) acquired her first Saluki in 1934 – Sheba Mazuri. Sheba totally captivated her owner with her charm, her gentle manners, her pretty ways of showing affection, and she started Mrs Angel on a lifelong involvement in the breed, an involvement which was to have an influence on Salukis all over the world. Mrs Angel kept both feathered and smooth Salukis in her kennels, believing that the smooth should not be neglected in favour of the feathered. In Britain five Mazuris became Champions, culminating with Ch. Mazuri Lail, a black-and-tan bitch, the second smooth, and last to date in Britain, to achieve this title. Mrs Angel's achievements might have been greater if disaster, in the form of distemper, had not struck her kennels in the forties and early fifties. In those days vaccines had not been developed, and the disease killed twenty dogs in two separate outbreaks during the late forties, and in 1950 she lost a further thirteen dogs. Despite these setbacks, Mrs Angel continued to breed. Mazuris were exported to Australia, Canada, Cuba, Finland, Germany, Holland, Italy, Sweden and the United States; many became Champions or produced progeny who became Champions. Today the name Mazuri continues through Mr Don Wieden, whose Sedeki Salukis now carry the prefix Sedeki-Mazuri. Mr Wieden is an American, who spent a period of time teaching in England. Before returning to America, he bred seven Champions and

Ch. Mazuri Lail (Ch. Mazuri Sedeki Tisa ex Mazuri Nosleen) Bred by Mrs Gwen Angel and owned by Mr J. Kenyon. The second smooth and last to date to achieve the title of Champion in Britain. Pearce.

Ch. Knightellington Melody (Ch. Knightellington Ibrahim ex Knightellington Zoulaira). Prolific winner in the show ring and on the coursing field.

showed three more to their titles. Mr Wieden has the distinction of being the only Saluki breeder to own dogs who have each obtained English, Canadian and American Championship titles: Eng. Am. Can. Ch. Jen Araby Mahal Bey of Sedeki (bred by Miss Wood, USA), Eng. Am. Can. Ch. Sedeki Falu, and Eng. Ir. Am. Can. Ch. Sedeki Barre. Barre won fourteen Challenge Certificates, nine Reserve Challenge Certificates. He became the Top Hound (all breeds) in Great Britain in 1977, and also acquired the title of Irish Champion. The Sedeki kennels continue the Mazuri tradition of breeding successfully both smooth and feathered Salukis in America.

The Knightellington Salukis span three generations of ownership: founded by Lady Gardner and followed by her daughter, Mrs Helen Baker, and her grand-daughter Mrs Rosemary Lewis with her husband Christopher. Lady Gardner's first Saluki was a birthday present from her children in 1931. She was a red grizzle called Nablous Dream of Delight, bred by Miss Joan Mitchell. Sadly, Dream died at an early age from distemper. In 1936 Lady Gardner purchased two Salukis from Miss Mitchell: Knightellington Nablous Sitara and Knightellington Nablous Selma. These became the foundation lines of the Knightellington kennel – a kennel that has excelled on both the coursing field and in the show ring, producing excellent dual-purpose hounds over the years. To date, seven Champions have been made up, and there have been many great coursing victories. Lady Gardner succeeded the Hon. Florence Amherst as President of the Saluki or Gazelle Hound Club in 1946, and retained that position until retiring in 1953. Lady Gardner believed that the Saluki should be a medium-sized hound with the grace and dignity of a gazelle, yet possessing the strength and agility to perform its tasks. The first Knightellington Champion was born in 1951 and the last to gain a title was in 1987 – a notable achievement by any standard. However, the record book is still not closed: both Mrs Baker and Mr and Mrs Lewis have continued the Knightellington tradition of producing dual-purpose hounds, winners both in the field and in the show ring.

During the forties and fifties Mrs E. Coston had considerable success with the Elhors kennel, with nine Champions listed in the Saluki Book of Champions. However, Kennel Club archives reveal that one of her accredited Champions, Gulshere Elhor, only received one Challenge Certificate – a mistake on the part of the Kennel Club, which had confused Ch. Gushan Elhor with Gulshere Elhor. In all, Mrs Coston bred thirty-four litters between 1943 and 1960, and she kept the majority of the Salukis in her own kennels. In 1945 Miss Vera Watkins (Windswift) used her demob money from the army to purchase her first Saluki, Zahara Zuleika bred by Mrs Franklin. Zuleika won two Challenge Certificates before her untimely death from dropsy. During 1950 Miss Watkins was presented with Sabbah (the

Ch. Bedouin Caliph (Bedouin Baytor Abdullah ex Bedouin Seawind Simyra). Top winning dog for five years and four times Saluki of the Year.

Ch. Burydown Freyha (Burydown Uki ex Burydown Saladina). Reserve Best in Show at Crufts, 1964.

morning) the Windswift, by the Ambassador to H. M. King Abdul Aziz Ibn Saud of Saudi Arabia. From a total of sixty-four English Champions made up since 1953, no fewer than twenty-nine carry his blood, besides many more in America, Scandinavia and other European countries. The Windswifts became particularly admired by coursing enthusiasts in California. In 1974 Mrs Watkins was presented with a trophy for the breeder of the best Saluki coursing bitch on the West Coast of America – Windswift Arif Bayt Shahin. The most notable dog from the Windswift Kennel is Ch. Windswift Al Caliph (Ch. Al Caliphs Alyfeh ex Windswift Khashil) owned by Mrs Deborah Copperthwaite. Ch. Windswift Al Caliph, a cream dog born in 1975, was remarkably successful: he is the current breed record holder, holding a total of thirty-five Challenge Certificates, all under different judges, and he is the winner of five Hound Groups and two Best in Shows.

Mrs Hope Waters' (Burydown) impressive influence on the breed, began in 1948 when she obtained a pair of Salukis of predominantly Mazuri breeding; unfortunately both died at an early age. Her foundation bitch was Burydown Saladina (from Amherstia and Sarona stock) who was mated to a German-bred dog, Burydown Uki, whose pedigree went back mainly to Sarona lines. The greatest single achievement of this kennel was when Ch. Burydown Freyha (Burydown Uki ex Burydown Saladina), holder of sixteen Challenge Certificates, was Reserve Best in Show at Crufts in 1964. Three other Salukis have won the Hound Group at Crufts, Ch. Almanza Kafiat in 1976, Ch. Shamal Kharaz in 1986 and Ch. Jazirat Bahiyya in 1991; but no Saluki has yet equalled Freyha's achievement, who reached the pinnacle of her success at the age of eight, proving the adage that the Saluki is a slow-maturing breed, and in the same triumphant year she won the Veteran Coursing Stakes in the field. Of all the many successful litters carrying the Burydown prefix, the "V" litter is generally considered to be one of the best. The litter of six black-and-tan or black-and-silver puppies, sired by Tabarka Sirocco out of Ch. Burydown Inanna, was born in 1967. Valmiki gained six Challenge Certificates, Vasara won seven Challenge Certificates for Mrs Christina Ormsby, and Vasha became an International Champion with Mr Tim Teillers (Samoems) in Holland. To date, Mrs Waters has bred a record number of twenty-five British Saluki Champions, and an innumerable number of overseas Champions. The kennel has also had considerable success on the coursing field. The first Champion to be bred by this kennel was Ch. Burydown Asphodel (Burydown Uki ex Burydown Saladina) born in 1951, and the latest Champion is Ch. Burydown Qabillah, born in 1985. Mrs Waters moved to Canada in 1988, but the prefix continues through her daughter Mrs Tessa Abbott. Many current breeders are indebted to Mrs Waters' breeding programme, and her stock has been the foundation for many Saluki kennels, including ourselves with Ch.

A group of Daxlore Salukis (left to right) :Beth of Daxlore 1CC 4RCCs. Ch. Alexandra of Daxlore 18CCs 4RCCs, Ch. Seamist of Daxlore 3CCs 1RCC and Ch. Alexis of Daxlore 4CCs 8RCCs.

Burydown Nazreen. Another well-known line to appear during the fifties was the Daxlores, whose prefix belongs to Mrs Skelton-Fortune. Thirteen British Champions emerged from this kennel, the most notable being Ch. Starbelle of Daxlore (Ch. Tahawi Euripides ex Ch. Seamist of Daxlore). Starbelle, an extremely elegant cream, won twenty-nine Challenge Certificates, and she still holds the breed record for the most tickets won by a Saluki bitch. Daxlore dogs have also gained their titles in Australia, Denmark, Finland, Sweden, Norway, Hong Kong, Portugal and America. Mrs Skelton-Fortune is no longer active in breeding, but the Daxlores continues through David and Helen Graham, who now share a joint interest in the prefix.

Miss Mary Long entered Salukis in the late fifties under her Amena (Arabic for faithful) prefix. Her foundation lines were Burydown, Windswift, Mazuri and Daxlore. From the onset, Miss Long's preoccupation was to breed Salukis with good movement; glamour, in her own words, could be added later. The kennel produced seven Champions; perhaps the most famous was her cream bitch, Ch. Amena Morning Glory (Ch. Almanza Kafiat ex Ch. Amena Joy).

The Tahawis, owned by the celebrated All-Rounder judge Mr Terry Thorn, became well established by the mid-sixties. His first Saluki, Windswift Rahman, was

Ch. Windswift Al Caliph (Ch. Al Caliphs Alyfeh ex Windswift Khashil). Breed record holder with 35CCs, all awarded under different judges.

purchased in 1959 from Miss Vera Watkins. Between 1962 and 1973, Mr Thorn bred twenty-six litters, ten of his dogs became British Champions and many more gained their titles overseas. Before he retired from breeding to concentrate on his judging appointments, Mr Thorn had the distinction of owning seven Champions all living under one roof.

Mr Ernest Tebbs' foundation bitch was Ch. Asphodel Almanza, bred by Jean Burns. Almanza become so well known within the breed with her successes in the show ring – winning nine Challenge Certificates – and her outstanding ability in the coursing field, that Mr Tebbs decided to adopt her name as his prefix (Almanza is also a village in Spain). Almanza was mated to Ch. Bedouin Caliph in 1969 and produced the legendary Ch. Almanza Kafiat. Kafiat, a fawn dog with black ear fringes, was well balanced both on the move and in conformation. He won twenty-four Challenge Certificates, sixteen Reserve Challenge Certificates, went Best in Show four times (including the Saluki or Gazelle Hound Club Championship Show), and won the Hound Group at Crufts in 1976. He took honours in numerous coursing stakes, and won the Sandpiper Trophy for the top show/coursing Saluki on three occasions. He went on to sire ten British Champions. The Almanza kennel has produced seven British Champions to date, one of the most recent being Ch. Almanza Magdiel, who went Best in Show at the Scottish Hound Association Championship Show in 1988.

Mrs Deborah Copperthwaite started her famous Al Caliph kennels in the sixties. Her first Saluki, Ch. Bedouin Caliph, was purchased in 1964 and won twenty-eight Challenge Certificates, thirteen Reserve Challenge Certificates, plus many more important wins. Ch. Bedouin Caliph, bred by Mrs Lucas and Mrs James, was an outstanding cream dog with tremendous presence and excellent conformation who moved with a lovely, lifting and effortless movement. Another outstanding dog owned by this kennel was Ch. Windswift Al Caliph, bred by Miss Vera Watkins. Ch. Windswift Al Caliph is the breed record holder with thirty-five Challenge Certificates. Mrs Copperthwaite has established the Al Caliphs as one of the leading lines within Britain, and has recently produced smooth lines to add to her feathered types. The kennel holds over one hundred Challenge Certificates, has bred nine British Champions, and has been the top kennel within the breed nearly every year for the past ten years. No doubt the Al Caliphs will continue to flourish and the record books will have to be rewritten.

The Geldara Salukis owned by Miss Sonia Lambrinudi have the distinction of producing five Champions from the five litters bred under this prefix – a feat most breeders would be proud of. Three Champions have been bred by Misses Chanter and Davies of the Chandav prefix – the lovely red bitch Ch. Rachel of Chandav (Ch.

*Ch. Rachel of Chadnav (Ch. Almanza Kafiat ex Almanza Asheba) 8CCs and
5 RCCs, winner of the Saluki Club show points trophy for top bitch in 1975/76.*

Almanza Kafiat ex Almanza Asheba), who lived to the grand age of eighteen and a
half years; Ch. Timotheus of Chandav (Ch. Al Caliphs Alyfeh ex Ch. Rachel of
Chandav) and Ch. Uri of Chandav (Ch. Amena Lucifer ex Tabitha of Chandav).
Timotheus, "Timo", is probably the most notable of this handsome trio, having a
marvellous show career and also being a predominant sire. He was the Top Saluki
Stud Dog 1985, 1986 and 1987, and many of his offspring are currently having
considerable success in the show ring.

Mrs Christina Ormsby, of the Yazid Salukis, used Ch. Burydown Vasara as her
foundation bitch, a Saluki who excelled both in the show ring and on the coursing
field. Mrs Ormsby's first litter was from Vasara to Ch. Burydown Pasha. The most
outstanding puppy from this litter was Am. Ch. Yazid Abqari, owned by Norma and
Leslie Everett, USA. Abqari gained his title before he was two years of age, and has
sired or been the grandsire of sixteen Champions. From the same litter Mrs Ormsby
kept Ashiqa, who was subsequently mated to Ch. Geldara Baryton and produced Ch.
Yazid Chehella Maria, winner of four Challenge Certificates and two Reserve
Challenge Certificates, Junior Warrant, and the first Saluki puppy to win Best Puppy
in Show at an all breeds Championship Show over three days. Chehella was also
extremely successful on the coursing field, winning both the prestigious Cleve Cup

Ch. Almanza Kafiat (Ch. Bedouin Caliph ex Ch. Asphodel Almanza. A true dual-purpose hound, excelled in the show ring and on the coursing field.

(two years running) and the Kerrison Trophy in the same year – a feat equalled only by one other Saluki since coursing commenced in 1928. Mrs Ormsby also owned Ch. Yazid Burydown Yehudi bred by Mrs Hope Waters, who was one of the outstanding coursing Salukis in the history of the breed. Four home-bred Champions have been made up under the Yazid prefix, including Ch. Yazid Ghanayena (Ch. Timotheus of Chandav ex Ch. Yazid Chehella) 13 CCs, 10 RCCs and top Saluki of the Saluki or Gazelle Hound Club 1984/85. Numerous wins have also been recorded on the coursing field for this kennel.

Mrs Jeanna Jaques (Classicus) resumed residence in Britain during the late seventies, returning with Burydown Iphigenia (Fudge) along with her other Salukis. "Fudge", bred by Mrs Hope Waters, was soon to gain her title. She was an outstanding cream bitch of the highest quality, won twenty-four Challenge Certificates, eleven Reserve Challenge Certificates, one Hound Group, and became the dam of eight Champions overall. Her daughter, Ch. Classicus Cassandara won sixteen Challenge Certificates and went Best in Show at the Hound Association of Scotland's Championship Show in 1986. So far, three Champions have been bred from the Classicus kennel.

In recent years there has been a proliferation of kennels that have achieved success

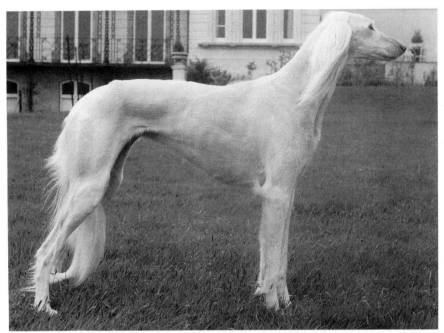

Ch. Burydown Iphigenia (Ch. Al Caliphs Alyfeh ex Ch. Burydown Xenia).
An exquisite cream who won 24 CCs and 11 RCCs and one Hound Group.

Ch. Saklawi Bishah of Mabrooka (Ch. Burydown Mubarak ex Mabrooka
Binaya of Saklawi) 13CCs and 2RCCs, Reserve Best in Show at
Richmond Championship Show in 1990.

Ch. Tahawi Belinda (Windswift Rahman ex Susha Riza) Brood Bitch of the Year 1968/69.

Ch. Yazid Ghaneyna (Ch. Timotheus of Chandav ex Ch. Yazid Chehella Maria) 13 CCs and 10RCCs.

Ch. Seafleet Kismet (Ch. Almanza Kafiat ex Seafleet Granada) 12 CCs 8 with BOB, the first being at Crufts 1977 where she was in the last five in the Hound Group.

Ch. Shamal Kharaz (Ch. Jeddah Al Caliphs ex Sedeki Tamineh of Shamal) 10CCs and 7RCCs and winner of the Hound Group at Crufts in 1986.

with their breeding programmes in Britain: Mr and Mrs Davies of the Lusaki prefix have, so far, bred five Champions. Mrs Zola Rawson of Mumtaz Salukis, has bred four Champions. Mrs Payne and Mr Beeley, together with Mr and Mrs John Walton Haddon with the Ilsham prefix, have bred three Champions. Mr and Mrs Cotterill (Miskanda), Mr and Mrs Kendall (Gulzar), Mr and Mrs Stansfield (Ishieya), Mr and Mrs Shellard (Seafleet) have also bred three Champions. Mesdames Lucas and James (Bedouin) have bred two Champions, including the famous Ch. Bedouin Caliph. The contemporary trend is for people to breed a litter once every three to four years to cater for their own show requirements; many have been successful with this policy and some outstanding hounds have been produced, namely: Ch. Shamal Kharaz (Ch. Jeddah Al Caliphs ex Sedeki Tamineh of Shamal) 10CCs 7RCCs, bred and owned by Mrs Merchant Giles, winner of the Hound Group at Crufts in 1986 and at the Ladies Kennel Association 1985; Ch. Kasaque Ezekiel 9CCs and 11 RCCs (Ch. Shamal Kharaz ex Ch. Kasaque Dharmas), bred by Mr and Mrs Williams and owned by Mr and Mrs Spooner, winner of two Hound Groups; Ch. Pennyworth Katiya 11CCs 6RCCs and Ch. Pennyworth Riaz 9CCs 7RCCs (Ch. Shamal Kharaz ex Ch. Kaus Kezia), both bred by Mrs Perkins (Riaz is owned by Mrs Webb); Ch. Saklawi Bishah of Mabrooka (Ch. Burydown Mubarak ex Mabrooka Binaya of Saklawi) 13CCs 2RCCs, bred by Mr and Mrs Wright and owned by Mr and Mrs Macdonald, Reserve Best in Show at Richmond 1990; and Ch. Jazirat Bahiyya (Jazirat Ariba ex Ch. Burydown Nazreen) 9CCs 9RCCs, bred and owned by Mr and Mrs Allan, Best in Show at the Saluki or Gazelle Hound Club Championship Show 1990 and winner of the Hound Group at Crufts 1991.

Chapter Four

STARTING IN THE BREED

When you buy a dog, you are making a commitment to that dog for the extent of its life. You are responsible for all its basic needs, providing the food, exercise and companionship, which will ensure that it lives a happy and healthy life. This is a lifetime obligation, and therefore the decision to buy a dog should not be taken lightly. Do not fall into the trap of buying on impulse. Before entering into this partnership, you must consider whether the Saluki is suitable for your lifestyle. The first step is to make sure you can afford to own this breed. As well as the purchase price, you must take into account the weekly food bill, veterinary fees and third party insurance cover, as you are liable under law for any damage or accidents that your dog may inadvertently cause. Your house must be large enough to accommodate a big dog, and the garden must be adequately fenced – at least five to six feet high. You must make sure you have enough time for its basic training, grooming and general care.

The Saluki is, paradoxically, both an easy and a difficult dog to own. If you are

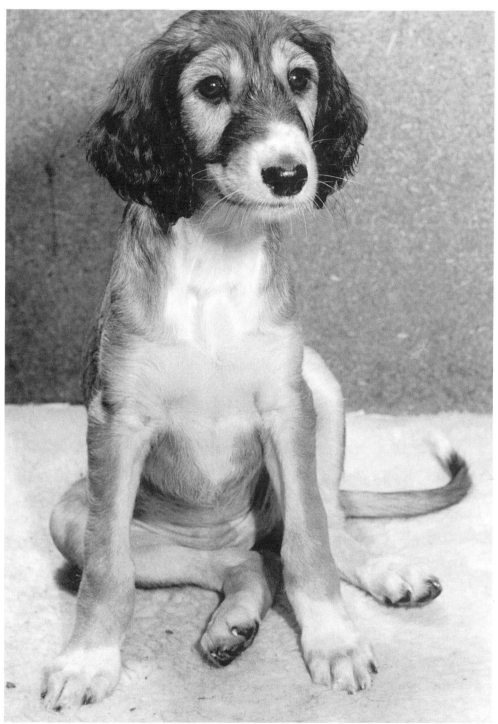

A bright and alert puppy of around seven weeks.

looking for an obedient lap-dog, one that will obey your every instruction, then the Saluki is not for you. They are highly independent, intelligent and faithful companions. However, they are running hounds with a highly in-bred instinct to chase anything that moves, and this is combined with an independence of spirit and mind. This is part of the Saluki's charm and fascination, but you have to be prepared for it. The Saluki also has a habit of choosing its owner, and it will usually select one human in every household who they respect and adopt as their peer leader. You have no choice – the choice is theirs. Before finally deciding on buying a Saluki, read as much as you can about the breed. Visit a few dog shows, and talk to the exhibitors about the pros and cons of ownership. Saluki owners and breeders will be only too pleased to give you advice and answer any questions. If possible, try to visit a breeder's house so that you can see the Saluki in the "home environment". If you haven't been put off after all this, you can count yourself as yet another that has succumbed to the Saluki's charms! However, there are still many important decisions to be made.

PUPPY OR ADULT?

Ideally, you should raise your dog from puppyhood. It is an undeniable pleasure to watch the dog grow up and develop from a lively pup into a mature and dignified Saluki. The partnership that is formed in those formative months of development will become one of the most rewarding canine relationships you will ever enter into. If you do not have sufficient time to devote to the rearing, feeding and training needs of a puppy, you can consider obtaining an older dog. Some specialist breeders occasionally have adult dogs for sale. Alternatively, Saluki breed clubs, worldwide, operate a rescue system for dogs that need to be re-housed, and these "rescue dogs" can give you an excellent introduction to the breed.

MALE OR FEMALE?

The decision whether to buy a dog or a bitch can be very difficult. Most Saluki owners have their own preferences, both on sex and type. We own one dog, and the rest are bitches. Apart from an overt sexual desire during his adolescence, and the continual desire to mark his territory with smalls squirts of urine while on a walk, we have found our dog a most charming companion. We find his temperament more consistent than the bitches, but of course, we do have to keep him separated from any of our bitches when they are in season.

Perhaps the biggest drawback to owning a bitch is their reproductive cycle. When

It is much easier to obtain a feathered Saluki than one of the smooth variety.

The Saluki has a highly in-bred instinct to chase.

a bitch is in season, she will act as a magnet for all the canine Casanovas in the locality. The frequency of the season varies from bitch to bitch: we own bitches with a ten-monthly cycle, but on average it occurs every six months. The length of the season can also vary, although it is usually about twenty days in duration. During this period the bitch can be restless and unreliable, and the small deposits of blood that she leaves around the house need constant cleaning up. Another problem that can ensue from oestrus is the false or phantom pregnancy: this is when the bitch will go through the whole reproductive process of having imaginary puppies, carrying them, nesting, and even providing milk for them. This can be a very disturbing time for the bitch, and it requires great patience and understanding from the owner.

SMOOTH OR FEATHERED?

This decision is purely subjective, based on your own personal preference. If you favour the smooth variety, you will have great difficulty obtaining this type in Britain, as very few are available. However, in America, the smooth enjoys a greater degree of popularity.

WHERE TO BUY?

When purchasing a puppy, you should always buy from an accredited Saluki breeder. If in doubt, phone the secretary of a Saluki breed club. Responsible breeders are anxious to find good permanent homes for their stock, so don't be surprised if you have to answer a series of questions regarding your reasons for wanting a Saluki. This is understandable; the breeder is not prying, but merely ensuring that you fully understand the problems of Saluki-ownership, and that the new home is suitable. For example, there should be someone at home all day, or periodically throughout the day, both to develop a relationship with the new puppy (dogs get lonely too), and to give it a chance to become house-trained. All breeders, without fail, will ask you about the size of your garden and whether it is properly fenced. The last point is most important – you don't want to lose the new addition to your family within the first week. As the prospective purchaser, you will have the opportunity to formulate your own opinion of the breeder's stock. If the dogs are hospitable, clean, and in good condition, then it is a fair bet that the puppies will be equally well cared for. If the litter has already been born, then you may get the opportunity of seeing the dam with the puppies.

CHOOSING YOUR PUPPY

Unless you are very lucky, you will have to wait for your puppy. The length of time will depend on the popularity of the breeder you have chosen. The more popular kennels, and particular matings, will probably have a waiting list of prospective owners. The breeder is likely to have made some arrangements with customers before the litter is born, such as allocating who will have the pick of litter or the pick of the best opposite sex. After the puppies have been born, the breeders will grade each one, based on their own experience and knowledge. It is quite normal for a variation of prices to be levied within the litter – puppies are usually evaluated on their perceived quality and expectations. Breeders will be honest about each pup's potential because it is in their own interest to be so. If a puppy is sold as a pet, it will naturally cost less than the pick of litter. As far as you are concerned, it will be the best puppy in the litter, and it may even prove to be a winner. We know of several Saluki puppies who were originally sold as pets and have been successfully shown in the show ring; one even went on to become a Champion. Whatever the pedigree of the sire or dam, it may not be possible to breed a Champion in every litter.

Obviously, some litters will have a greater potential than others, and a discerning purchaser can significantly increase the odds by selecting their breeder wisely. However, most breeders can do no more than guarantee a puppy has the potential of being worthy of serious showing, at the time of the sale. The rest is up to you. If you rear the puppy correctly, providing the right exercise and training, there is no reason why its early promise should not be realised in the show ring. You harvest what you sow.

Saluki puppies should look plump, but not pot-bellied, and they should have plenty of bone. They tend to look more like baby Labradors Knobbly knees are a sign that the puppy will grow into a good-sized hound. Watch the puppies playing and see how they interact with each other. The young puppies should be friendly and seeking attention. The natural aloofness of the Saluki develops with maturity and when it is settled with its future owner. Remember when you visit a litter that puppies tend to play in short bursts of violent activity, so the one that is asleep in the corner may be tired from rushing about just before you came in; it is not necessarily reserved or nervous. The puppy's eyes should be bright and alert, the skin and ears should be clean and smell pleasant. Look at any faeces that may be in the pen – they should be well formed. Check the teeth for bite, and if it is a male puppy, ensure that he has two testicles fully descended into the scrotum.

COLLECTING THE PUPPY

Most breeders allow the puppies to leave their kennels when they are between eight and ten weeks old. Your puppy should be fit and healthy and, for very little extra cost, you can ask the breeder to provide a veterinary certificate of health. Try to collect your puppy during the morning; this will give you time to settle the pup into its new home. We normally bath the puppy and give it a good run, prior to collection. We also provide a diet sheet, which details the type of food as well as the times of day the puppy is used to being fed, together with about two days supply of food. This ensures that the diet is not dramatically changed when the puppy is adjusting to a new environment.

The puppies will have started a worming programme, and they will probably have had the first of a two-part vaccination course against distemper, hardpad, hepatitis, leptospirosis and canine parvovirus. The breeder should provide details of the products used and other relevant information so the programme can be continued. Make sure you check whether the first set of vaccinations has been given. If not, you will have to arrange with your own veterinary surgeon to start the course straight away. You will also be given a signed copy of the dog's pedigree, a detailed receipt,

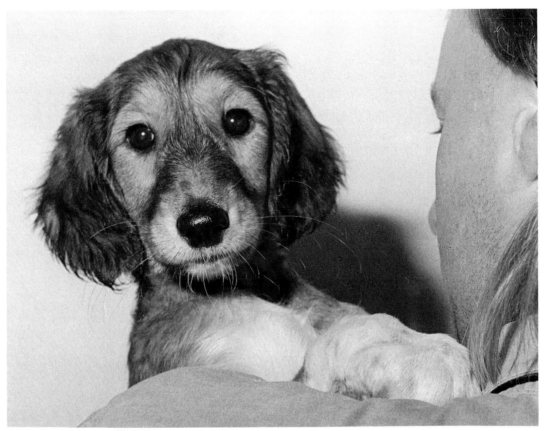

A puppy leaves home, all ready to start its new life.

and the Kennel Club registration certificate, on which the transfer of ownership section has been signed by the breeder. You will need to sign and complete the form before sending it to the Kennel Club with a cheque for the transfer fee of £6. Some breeders may ask you to sign a basic contract, which will set out the terms and conditions of the sale. If this is required you will also retain a copy.

The puppy's first few days and nights in the new home are often quite traumatic, and the new owner will need time and patience to help the puppy to adapt to its new surroundings. Always remember, if you are concerned in any way, the breeder is only a phone call away, and will be only too pleased to offer advice.

Young puppies tend to play in short bursts of about half an hour.

Chapter Five

CARING FOR YOUR SALUKI

Before your puppy arrives home, you should have made certain preparations. First and foremost, your garden must be made Saluki-proof with adequate fencing between five and six feet in height. The Saluki grows into quite a tall dog (24-28 inches), and some are very good jumpers; the young puppy will also be a very good escape artist. The pup will need a bed of its own; this is essential, as it will contribute to the puppy developing a sense of security in its new home. It is bound to miss the warmth and companionship of its mother and siblings, so anything that will lessen this initial trauma is a help. The bed doesn't need to be elaborate: a cardboard box with one of the sides cut down, and a blanket to sleep on, is perfectly adequate to start with. Some people put a hot-water bottle wrapped in a towel under the blanket, to act as a surrogate mother. We have found that as soon as our dogs are house-trained, they swiftly disregard their bed and find their own place within the household; generally the settee or an armchair – always the most comfortable place they can discover. We have bean-bags scattered around for emergency seating –

Most Salukis prefer to eat their food from a dish raised off the ground.

usually ours! The first night is commonly feared by most new owners, and almost inevitably, your first few nights sleep will be disturbed, as the puppy will be "homesick" and will cry. Try to resist the temptation to take the pup into the bedroom, unless you want it to sleep with you forever. If you ignore the crying, the puppy will soon settle down. Be conciliatory, do not punish or admonish it – that will only increase its insecurity. Although the puppy may appear delighted with its new home, it is bound to encounter some form of inner stress at the change of environment. Refrain from inviting too many people to see your new acquisition for a few days until it has had time to settle down and become familiar with the immediate family. After this initial acclimatisation period, the more human contact the dog experiences, the better its temperament should be. The Saluki is a gentle and sensitive dog, one which can easily become timid or nervous if it doesn't receive enough human companionship and understanding. Socialisation is therefore vital, and the earlier it starts, the easier it will be for both you and your puppy. It is a good idea to get your puppy used to wearing a collar in the house from an early stage. This should be light and comfortable, and then the pup will scarcely notice it.

It is essential that you make an appointment with your vet as soon as possible, as the worming and vaccination programmes started by the breeder must be continued. Until the puppy has completed its vaccination courses, it carries little or no

The Saluki loves to run free.

immunity from disease and must be kept isolated from possible infection. On your first visit to the surgery, we suggest that you keep the puppy in the car until the vet is ready to see you. Never take the puppy into the waiting room or put it on the floor; there might be sick dogs or germs around. The veterinary surgeon will advise you when it is safe to introduce the puppy to the outside world; this is usually about two weeks after the final inoculation has been given. He will also tell you about future vaccination requirements; a booster is normally required every year.

Young puppies tend to play for about half-an-hour, and then sleep for an hour-and-a-half throughout the day. A young puppy, like a child, needs long periods of rest for the development of a strong and healthy body. After the first couple of days, you will probably be grateful for the rest periods, as play-times are hectic and demanding. Young Salukis are naturally inquisitive, boisterous and full of mischief. We have a range of "toys", so that the pup has something to amuse itself with during its play period. Although there are many commercial toys available, our pups always seem to get most enjoyment from tearing up old newspapers, shaking an old pair of tights, chasing a ball about, or chewing on something solid.

The puppy should be fed at regular intervals with small amounts of food, four times a day. The first meal should be given early in the morning, and the last at bedtime. The dog will also require a separate feeding and drinking bowl. It is best to keep this on a piece of newspaper to begin with as spills are common. We would strongly recommend that you continue following the diet sheet provided by the breeder, only introducing new foods, if desired, after the first two weeks. Then, substitute a little of the new food gradually, mixing it with the food the dog is used to. Never change the diet all in one go. During puppyhood, there should be plenty of milk, cooked eggs (uncooked white of an egg is unsuitable), cereal and meat on the menu. Don't forget to increase the amount of food as the puppy grows. While it is growing it will consume about twice as much in a day as an adult Saluki. Fresh water should always be available.

Our own puppies are fed on a diet that Mrs Hope Waters (Burydown) supplied when we purchased a puppy from her, and it has stood us in good stead when rearing our own litters. From weaning, they are fed four meals a day: the first meal is either Farex or Ready-Brek, soaked in milk with a spoonful of honey, the second meal is raw meat followed with goat's milk, the third meal is egg custard, and supper consists of fine wholemeal biscuit soaked in gravy with a little cooked meat. After the puppy is twelve weeks of age, one of the milk meals is cut out. At twenty-four weeks the meals are reduced to two: breakfast and supper, and from about forty-eight weeks onwards we give one main meal, which is a combination of Laughing Dog Natural 19 (our only change from the original list), meat (either cooked or Pedigree Chum) and gravy, with a Laughing Dog wholemeal biscuit for breakfast. We have found this product range suitable for our dogs' needs, contributing to their overall health and well-being. Other manufacturers make similar products, all scientifically balanced, and all claiming their own particular advantages. As a general rule, find one which suits your dog, in terms of good digestive function and satisfactory growth – then keep to it. Unlike humans, variety is not necessary in a dog's diet; continual changes of menu do not suit them. If changes to the diet have to be made, introduce them gradually over a two to three week period. A fully-grown, healthy Saluki should have its hip bones showing, and two to three ribs just visible beneath the skin. The flesh should be firm, well-muscled with no excess fat, and the coat should have a healthy sheen.

A Saluki's ear-feathering can start to grow quite quickly, though the length and speed of growth varies enormously. As the feathering gets longer it tends to hang down into the food dish, making the hair both greasy and sticky. The feathering can also get stuck on a bone, or fall on to the surfaces of large biscuits and get chewed by the back teeth in the biting process. To avoid this problem, you can either purchase a snood or cut off a length of old nylon tights and slip them over the dog's head at meal-times. Salukis have long legs and a long neck, and so they prefer to eat their food from a dish raised off the ground. Both puppies and adult dogs enjoy bones. They help with puppy's teething, they keep an adult's teeth clean and their gums in good condition. Avoid small bones (which can get stuck in the mouth if swallowed), cooked bones (which tend to crack), and bones from poultry (which splinter into dangerous sharp pieces). We usually let a dog have a bone for a short period, and then take it away. A good size marrow bone will last about a week, if it is given for about thirty minutes a day. After six or seven days, throw the bone away and get a new one.

House-training is usually the foremost priority with every new owner – everyone wants their puppy to be "clean" as soon as possible. However, do not expect too much, too soon. An eight-week-old puppy has very little bladder control, and an initial satisfactory result is usually achieved by accident, rather than by design. Puppies should have the opportunity to relieve themselves after every meal, and after waking from a long sleep. Take the puppy out into the garden to a chosen spot, and stay with them until they either urinate or defecate. Always encourage the puppy to perform, and praise a successful result. It is entirely useless to put the puppy out on its own, it will have no idea what it is expected to do. You are bound to have some mistakes at first, but repetition and association, together with patience and persistence will ultimately produce the desired results. Never scold a mistake; the puppy has to learn to control its bowels, exactly like a child. Be patient, and give love and understanding. Anger will only make the puppy feel rejected, isolated and confused. It is unrealistic to expect one hundred per cent cleanliness before about six months – if that seems too long, remember a child takes much longer.

It is advisable to introduce your puppy to travelling in a car at an early age. Some dogs take to cars immediately, others are car-sick within the first mile or so. If your dog seems to have a problem, tolerance and perseverance are perhaps the major essentials of success. Take the puppy on short trips at first, building up the distance gradually, until your dog becomes familiar with this mode of transport. It is best to do this when the pup has had a chance to digest its food. All too often, people will feed their dog and then take it off on a journey, and then they are surprised when the puppy is sick all over the seat of the vehicle. Try to make the dog associate the car with something pleasant, like a short walk, so that it connects the outing with nice things rather than a trip to the vet. Car sickness is a form of nerves and can be overcome with acclimatisation. Sedatives can be used successfully, but these should only be given on veterinary advice. It is essential that you never leave your dog alone in a car for long periods, especially in hot weather. On a very warm day, even if the windows are open, the interior of the car heats up like a greenhouse, and dogs can easily suffer from heatstroke or dehydration, and they can die from this in a remarkably short length of time.

Water holds an irresistable attraction.

The first year of a Saluki's life is crucial to its development, it needs both affection and a sense of security. Salukis make delightful companions, and they blossom when they live in the house with the family. Apart from their extreme elegance and aristocratic demeanour, they are quiet and unobtrusive animals. Never be tempted to over-exercise your puppy within the first nine to twelve months of its life. All our puppies are allowed total freedom to run around our garden, until they decide that enough is enough. Our adults are not allowed to run with them, as this will only encourage the puppy to over-exert itself. We never take our puppies for walks until they are about six months of age, and then limit them to a short distance. The bones and muscles are still developing, and if a puppy is given too much exercise in the early months, longer term problems can develop, such as deformity of tendons and ligaments. It is difficult to specify exact amounts of exercise for individual dogs – just try to gauge when your dog has had enough. As a general rule, never walk or run your dog into exhaustion; just try to take the edge off their energy. We often wonder how much of the poor movement seen in the show ring can be attributed to excessive exercise at a vulnerable age.

Of course, our adult Salukis get much more exercise – usually four to six miles of road-walking every day, plus a free run. We are fortunate in having a large garden, and a farmer who allows us access to her fields. The latter often produces an

Surfing in the USA.   *Susan Schroder.*

unsolicited course, much to the delight of the dogs. Some Saluki owners seem reluctant to let their dogs run free, because they are concerned about catching them. Most Salukis run in a large elliptical shape, and they like to keep their owner in sight; every now and then stopping to check the whereabouts of their custodian. It is relatively rare for a Saluki to take off in a straight line and disappear over the horizon, although it is bound to happen if they are in hot pursuit of a quarry. However, they have strong homing instincts and will nearly always return to the point where they were unleashed. We have owned Salukis that are difficult to catch, as well as the more biddable types, and we can appreciate people's concern about letting their dogs loose. Our first Saluki was allowed to run free from an early age in a variety of situations and locations. At first she returned to heel quite easily, but later on as her confidence developed, she became more adventurous and only deigned to be caught when she had had enough of her freedom. Even the mode of capture was on her terms. It was too much for her pride to come straight up to either of us, and she wouldn't stand still and let us go to her. Oh no! She had to pretend that she still didn't want to be caught, and after playing the game for a little while, she would eventually allow herself to be cornered in a position where the only escape was to come to us. It was good fun and she thoroughly enjoyed it; for us, however, it was sheer frustration and we were overwhelmed by a total feeling of hopelessness. Eventually, when she reached the age of three, she became much more biddable, and we were able to capture her almost on demand.

Learning from experience, we now only release our dogs within fields that have clearly defined boundaries, at the same time ensuring that there are no farm animals in the adjoining fields. We also let our dogs run on deserted beaches, which tends to be confined to the winter months. That can also prove hazardous. Last year we were travelling to a Championship Dog Show in Edinburgh, and after driving some two hundred miles, we decided to exercise our dogs on the sands, just north of Newcastle. All was well for the first ten minutes or so, until a couple of seagulls decided to tease one of our dogs, swooping in low just in front of her to encourage the chase. They then proceeded to skim low along the sands, flying just fast enough to keep out of the reach of our chasing hound. Carefully, as if by intent, they led her out and into the sea. We stood helpless as our carefully bathed and manicured Saluki ran deeper and deeper into the crashing waves and surf. She disappeared underwater, and it seemed like hours before she surfaced. Fortunately, she realised she was beaten, but it was a long hard swim before she reached the safety of the shore. The moral to this little episode is that the Saluki is a free spirit, with a mind of its own. When a dog is unleashed, the owner has little or no control, especially if there is something to chase. Obedience owners will throw up their hands in horror at this statement, but nevertheless, it is true. A Saluki will obey commands within the confines of training classes, but it will often ignore the same commands when it has the freedom of the wide open spaces. All you can do is to be patient and have confidence, because the Saluki will always eventually return – its just a matter of time. Losing your temper will not yield results; it will probably make matters worse, as the Saluki will become apprehensive, and as a result, less co-operative. Most Salukis will normally return to their owner after burning off their energy, but others may go off looking for adventure, only returning at their own convenience.

If you have difficulty with catching your hound, try luring him with titbits. We have also had success by completely ignoring the dog's antics; the Saluki hates to be ignored, and therefore pretending not to be interested in their performance can sometimes induce a response. We either sit down with our backs to the dog, or pretend to walk away. It will then try to attract our attention by running close to us, or even coming up beside us and giving us a quick nudge – then all that is required is a skilful rugby tackle! Although all of this sounds horrendous, it should be emphasised that it doesn't happen every time the dog is allowed to run free, and the thrill and beauty of seeing your Saluki at full stretch is indeed poetry in motion, and is well worth all the frustrations that might follow. The sight of a Saluki doing what it likes best – running at full stretch, a large grin on its face, ears swept back by the pressure of the wind, the aerodynamics of the gallop co-ordinating to perfection, and the tail sweeping first one way and then the other like a rudder – is a privilege to behold.

LEAD TRAINING

It is best to start work on this at an early stage. To begin with, the young puppy will try all sorts of antics to protest about this unusual form of restraint and enforced guidance. Titbits and words of praise will eventually persuade him to follow you around in roughly the direction you wish. Soon the puppy will learn to associate the lead with the pleasure of going for a walk, with the added bonus of investigating fresh territory. Never drag the puppy along, as this will only make him more apprehensive. If you see another dog on your walk, keep on walking, without making a deliberate ploy of avoiding the stranger. If a dog feels threatened, it could become aggressive as it gets older. Be cautious when you are introducing a young dog to traffic or to a crowd of people, and never take your puppy out until he is completely inoculated.

Initial training can start in the garden. Make sure you purchase a collar that fits (Salukis are very adept at escaping from a loose collar), and a lead of about five feet in length. Teach your puppy to walk beside you, at heel. If the dog starts to pull, give a short, sharp jerk on the collar, with the command "heel". If the dog responds, reward him, if not, jerk him harder until he receives the message. You are taking the dog for a walk, not vice versa. Failure to win this battle will lay the foundation for the commonest of bad habits – pulling on the lead. Bad habits never go away, they just get worse

TEACHING GOOD BEHAVIOUR

Like all learning processes, the sooner you start the sooner you will see results. However, do not expect too much too soon. Everything concerned with the socialisation of your puppy takes time, tolerance, and mountains of patience. A puppy is like a baby, and it cannot be expected to run before it can walk.There is an awful lot for it to learn before it can become a fully integrated and obedient member of the family. The new puppy, may look adorable and lovable, but do not be deceived – there is a stubborn intelligence developing, and you must, kindly but firmly, ensure that it realises you are the master from the beginning.

During the first few weeks, restrict your puppy's world to an area that is easily cleaned, and where someone can keep an eye on it for most of the time. It is no use giving your puppy the freedom of the house, and then complaining about the trail of messes it leaves in its wake. The kitchen is an ideal place to confine a new pup during the day. In the evening it can join the rest of the canine family in the lounge, until bedtime.

Teach your Saluki the simple rudiments of obedience training, such as: the recall, "heel", "stop", "stay", "wait" and "lie down". Although, this might be of little use when the dog is free-running, most Salukis will respond to basic orders in a controlled environment. Always call or give your commands in an authoritative but quiet manner, using the same word. Do not shout, unless you are trying to avert an imminent disaster! If you work on a daily training programme, you will win your dog's affection and loyalty from the start. Punishment has little value in basic training; the best approach is to praise when the command has been carried out successfully, and to withhold praise when the dog has failed to obey. With continual use, "good dog" and "bad dog" will become sufficient reward and punishment in themselves. The dog is a natural pack animal and if he accepts you as his pack leader, he will instinctively want to please. Hitting a dog for disobedience may get rid of your own frustrations, but it will only teach the dog to stay out of the range of your hands. Close contact and a good relationship are essential. Should you require to discipline your dog for a serious misdemeanour, grasp the skin at the back of the neck with both hands and raise the dog slightly off the ground, give it a good shake and stare into its eyes while giving a harsh verbal "no". Under normal circumstances, a short gruff "no", followed by a loud clap of the hands is usually sufficient. The Saluki is usually obedient and is eager to appease – so long as you have gained their respect and affection in the first place. It is essential that you only reprimand the dog at the time of the offence; it is no good calling it away from doing something naughty, and then telling it off – the puppy will think it has been punished for coming to you when it has been called. If you should require professional advice regarding training, dog training classes can be rewarding and good fun; equally your dog, allowing for its natural aloofness, will also have the opportunity to mix with different breeds.

GROOMING

The Saluki has virtually no "doggy odour" and does not moult like other canine breeds, although some hair is shed. It is predominantly a smooth-coated breed, and so lengthy grooming sessions are not necessary. A firm bristle brush (not nylon) used daily, to remove any dead hair, is usually sufficient; it also keeps the feathering free from unsightly tangles. Brush in long sweeping strokes following the lie of the

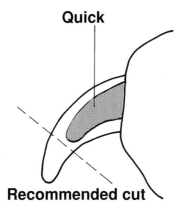

Quick

Recommended cut

Trimming nails

coat. Care should be taken when grooming the head and around other sensitive regions of the anatomy.

The nails should be checked on a weekly basis and trimmed as necessary. We use a guillotine-type of clippers on our dogs, holding the foot firmly and cutting just below the quick. With white nails you can easily see the tip of the nail, with black nails it is more difficult, so err on the side of caution. If you cut too high, the nail will bleed copiously; don't panic – apply a styptic pencil to the wound.

When we bathe our dogs we use our own bath and a mild "human" or "baby" shampoo. The procedure is very much like washing your own hair: soak the hair, apply shampoo and lather, rinse, apply a conditioner (optional), towel dry and complete drying with a hair dryer. The frequency of bathing is a matter of personal choice. It is also worth getting into the routine of checking your Saluki's ears about once a week for infection or an accumulation of wax. If the ears need cleaning, use cotton wool and a small amount of baby oil. Be careful not to probe into any part of the ear you cannot see. If the ear has an infection, consult your vet immediately. Similarly, never use ear drops or powders unless on professional advice.

Teeth should be checked frequently, and small amounts of tartar carefully removed with a moistened cotton-wool bud dipped in tooth powder. More stubborn tartar can be scraped, using a dentist's scaler; the best type is shaped like a tiny spoon. Scale from the gum towards the tip of the tooth, applying a certain amount of pressure – not a job for the faint-hearted. However, prevention is better than cure. If the teeth are brushed two to three times a week, paying special attention to where the gums and teeth meet, tartar should not develop and the gums will remain healthy. It is not necessary to clean the inside of the teeth (tongue-side) as these are cleansed naturally. It is rare for a dog to experience dental decay; dog's teeth are shaped for tearing and cutting rather than grinding, therefore particles of food do not tend to get lodged in the teeth.

Daily grooming of your Saluki helps to deepen mutual trust and understanding. Most dogs enjoy these sessions, and it gives you a good opportunity to check for any ailments. A well-groomed Saluki shows a pride of ownership, which is fitting to this true aristocrat of canine breeds.

Chapter Six

THE BREED STANDARD

The Saluki, like all pedigree dogs, is measured against a written description of what an ideal specimen should look like. The Breed Standard is a blueprint for judges, breeders, and anyone interested in the show ring. The original Breed Standard (still used by the American Kennel Club) was drawn up by founder members of the Saluki or Gazelle Hound Club. They mostly owned desert-bred Salukis and therefore had a detailed knowledge of the breed's natural habitat and its hunting origins. The standard of points, recognised by the Kennel Club in 1923, allowed for a variety of Saluki types, which reflected the hounds owned by the club members. This has stood the breed in good stead for some sixty-three years, and by and large, it has preserved the Saluki true to its original form.

THE AMERICAN KENNEL CLUB STANDARD
(The 1923 British Breed Standard)

HEAD: Long and narrow, skull moderately wide between the ears, not domed, stop not pronounced, the whole showing great quality. Nose black or liver.
EARS: Long and covered with long silky hair hanging close to the skull and mobile.

EYES: Dark to hazel and bright; large and oval, but not prominent.
TEETH: Strong and level.
NECK: Long, supple and well muscled.
CHEST: Deep and moderately narrow.
FOREQUARTERS: Shoulders sloping and set well back, well muscled without being coarse.
FORELEGS: Straight and long from the elbow to the knee.
HINDQUARTERS: Strong, hip bones set well apart and stifle moderately bent, hocks low to the ground, showing galloping and jumping power.
LOIN AND BACK: Back fairly broad, muscles slightly arched over loin.
FEET: Of moderate length, toes long and well arched, not splayed out, but at the same time not cat-footed; the whole being strong and supple and well feathered between the toes.
TAIL: Long, set on low and carried naturally in a curve, well feathered on the underside with long silky hair, not bushy.
COAT: Smooth and of a soft silky texture, slight feather on the legs, feather at the back of the thighs and sometimes with slight woolly feather on the thigh and shoulder.
COLOUR: White, cream, fawn, golden, red, grizzle and tan, tricolour (white, black and tan) and black and tan.
GENERAL APPEARANCE: The whole appearance of this breed should give an impression of grace and symmetry and of great speed and endurance coupled with strength and activity to enable it to kill gazelle or other quarry over deep sand or rocky mountains. The expression should be dignified and gentle, with deep, faithful, far-seeing eyes. Dogs should average in height from 23 to 28 inches and bitches may be considerably smaller, this being very typical of the breed.
SMOOTH VARIETY: In this variety the points should be the same with the exception of the coat, which has no feathering.

Reproduced by kind permission of the American Kennel Club

During the early 1980s the English Kennel Club embarked on a programme to unify all Breed Standards into a common format. Breed clubs were asked to prepare draft proposals: fundamentally their brief was to rearrange the existing text under standardised headings and to prepare new material for areas that had not been covered. In essence, the aim was to clarify the Breed Standard – not to change it. However, when the new Breed Standard was published by the Kennel Club in 1986, it was received with dismay by the majority of Salukiphiles. Instead of being a

simple textural rearrangement of the old standard, it contained alterations and additions which many felt could substantially change the Saluki as we know it today. Breed reaction was universal and worldwide in its condemnation. In Britain a petition was organised and signed by the majority of Saluki owners asking the Kennel Club to reinstate, wherever possible, the wording of the 1923 Breed Standard. As a result of all the protests, the Saluki or Gazelle Hound Club, in conjunction with the Northern Saluki Club, held a Special General Meeting in 1989 to formulate a revised standard. This new Breed Standard has been submitted to the Kennel Club and is currently being considered by the Breeds Standard Sub-Committee. It is hoped that the final outcome will be to the benefit of the Saluki, rather than a compromise of political issues. Those that Allah has created, let no man put asunder!

THE 1986 BRITISH BREED STANDARD

GENERAL APPEARANCE: Gives impression of grace and symmetry and of great speed and endurance, coupled with strength and activity. Expression: dignified and gentle with far-seeing eyes.

CHARACTERISTICS: Of great quality with unique shaped foot, necessary for hunting natural terrain.

TEMPERAMENT: Reserved with strangers but not nervous or aggressive. Dignified, intelligent and independent.

HEAD AND SKULL: Head long and narrow, skull moderately wide between ears, not domed, stop not pronounced, whole showing great quality. Nose black or liver.

EYES: Dark to hazel, bright, large and oval, not prominent.

EARS: Long and mobile, not too low set, covered with long silky hair, hanging close to skull. Bottom tip of leather reaches to corner of mouth when brought forward. Provided ear is covered with silky hair, which may grow only from top half, the standard is complied with, but longer hair also correct.

MOUTH: Teeth and jaws strong with a perfect, regular and complete scissor bite, i.e. the upper teeth closely overlapping the lower teeth and set square to the jaws.

NECK: Long, supple and well muscled.

FOREQUARTERS: Shoulders sloping and set well back, well muscled without being coarse. Chest deep and moderately narrow, when viewed from front not an inverted "V". Forelegs straight and long from elbow to wrist. Pasterns strong and slightly sloping. Not round boned. Humerus sloping slightly backwards.

BODY: Back fairly broad, muscles slightly arched over loin, but never roached backed. Brisket long and deep, not barrel-ribbed or slab-sided, with good cut-up. Sufficient length of loin important.

HINDQUARTERS: Strong hip bones set wide apart. Stifle moderately bent with well developed first and second thigh. Hocks low to the ground.

FEET: Strong and supple, of moderate length, toes slightly webbed, long and well arched, two inner toes considerably longer than two outer toes on all four feet. Not splayed out or cat-footed and feathered between toes. Front feet point forward at very slight angle when standing.

TAIL: Set on low from long and gently sloping pelvis. Carried naturally in curve. Well feathered on underside but not bushy. In adults not carried above line of back except in play. Tip reaching to hock.

GAIT/MOVEMENT: Light, lifting, effortless, showing both reach and drive, body lifting off ground with long, flat strides, not flinging itself forward. No hackney action or plodding.

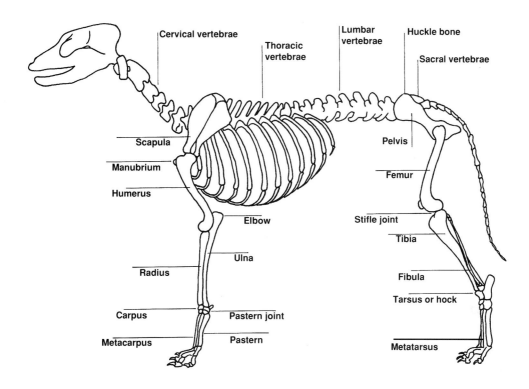

Skeletal structure.

COAT: Smooth, of silky texture, feathering on legs and back of thighs and between hock and heel. Puppies may have slight woolly feathering on thigh and shoulder. Feathering on throat permissible but not desirable. Smooth variety as above but without feathering.

COLOUR: White, cream, fawn, golden red, grizzle, silver grizzle, deer grizzle, tri-colour (white, black and tan), black and tan and variations of these colours, i.e. black fringed fawn, black fringed red not brindle.

SIZE: Dogs 58.4 - 71.1cm (23 - 28ins) at shoulders, bitches proportionately smaller.

FAULTS: Any departure from the foregoing points should be considered a fault and the seriousness with which the fault should be regarded should be in exact proportion to its degree.Note: Male animals should have two apparently normal testicles fully descended into the scrotum.

Reproduced by kind permission of the English Kennel Club.

JUDGING TO THE STANDARD

The dog show game, is exactly that: a game – one with an element of chance and a degree of luck. All exhibitors participate by testing their dog's beauty, prowess and conformation against other competitors. It enables breeders to present the results of their carefully selected breeding programme, and spectators have a chance to evaluate the dogs on show. It is a shop window, and judgements are made regarding the overall quality and standard of the breed on display. The "game" itself is governed by strict rules and procedures laid down by the Kennel Club, or other canine governing bodies. Handlers use their skill to present the dogs to their best advantage – disguising faults and emphasising virtues. It is enacted before an "expert of the breed" – a judge whose opinion is sought after, and hopefully valued. The judge's final decision may evoke delight, amazement, despair, or even anger. It will certainly provide the fancy with a talking point for the rest of the day.

The English Kennel Club publishes a *Guide to Judges*, which defines the obligations of a judge and the essential ingredients of competent judging. These are listed as:

BREED KNOWLEDGE: The most important single aspect of judging is knowledge of the breed to be judged and its standard. Judges must know the standard of the breed, fully understand its implications and be able to apply this knowledge. They should also be able to recognise breed type and have a basic knowledge of canine anatomy.

INTEGRITY: Judges must be honest and impartial, judging the dogs on merit.

TEMPERAMENT AND STAMINA: They should have a suitable temperament to judge and sufficient stamina for what can be a physically demanding task

This last point is more important than the novice judge might appreciate.The Saluki Club of America's Specialty Show in Lexington, Kentucky shows why stamina is essential. This show usually attracts an entry of between 400 and 500 Salukis and the officiating judge executes his or her assignment over three days. It is not a task for the faint-hearted.

That oft-quoted maxim "Beauty is in the eye of the beholder" is never more true than when it is applied to the art of judging. Judging is, and can only be, the subjective expression of an individual's personal opinion, based on their own knowledge, experience and interpretation of the Breed Standard. Today, few Saluki judges have any knowledge of the desert environment from which the Saluki originated, much less the qualities that the Arab sought from his fleet-footed hound. The Arab was not looking for a show beauty. His criterion was to breed an efficient hunting machine, swift and ruthless, with the modus operandi of catching "game for the pot." Out of this function he created, by chance, a dog of ethereal beauty, and one our founder members were so keen to protect when they formulated the 1923 Breed Standard.

Whether you are exhibiting, breeding or judging, the Breed Standard provides the objective framework of what constitutes the perfect Saluki. At dog shows, the judge is obliged to judge to the standard. Selection should be based on structure, movement, type, and the ability of the Saluki to perform its original function. The Saluki is a unique breed, and those characteristics and traits that keep it nonpareil should be uppermost in the judge's mind. It should also be remembered that there is more than one acceptable type allowed within the Breed Standard, and no type is more, or less, correct than the other. Of course, everyone has their own favourite, and obviously these are promoted within personal breeding programmes. When you are assessing a Saluki, great importance must be placed on correct conformation, balance and soundness, but it is type that keeps a Saluki a Saluki. Any dog can be a good physical specimen and yet be untypical of its breed. Type is therefore essential if we are to maintain and preserve the Saluki that we have inherited, largely unimpaired, from our forebearers.

The Breed Standard is open to personal analysis. It is very difficult to put into a few words a clear definition of what a dog should look like and how it should move, and so there will always be controversy over interpretation. The present Breed Standard gives a good guideline to the specialist judge, but it is very spartan in its description for those who are new to the breed. The following explanation of points is based on our own personal opinions, articles we have read and conversations with leading exponents within the breed.

HEAD ASSEMBLY

The head, as in most breeds, is one of the most important identifying characteristics of the Saluki. When analysing the head, it is essential to keep the total dog in mind. Each individual part of the Saluki is important to the overall balance and conformation, and each individual part contributes to the total picture. The Breed Standard allows for a wide range of sizes – 23 to 28 inches. It is, therefore, obvious that the size of head will vary from dog to dog, but they should remain in proportion to the overall assembly. When viewed from the side, the length of the foreface from the tip of the nose to the top of the stop should roughly equal the length of skull. The muzzle should taper towards the nose, and there should be sufficient underjaw. If the muzzle is too narrow, or the underjaw is weak, it displays a lack of power, which the Saluki needs in order to grab and kill its quarry. The skull should be refined and

Good head on a Saluki bitch.

moderately wide between the ears without being coarse or heavy. The Arabs called for a span of two fingers between the ears. The correct width of backskull also gives the triangular shape to the overall head when it is viewed from above.

The nose can be either black or liver. No preference is stated regarding Roman noses versus straight noses: those who select one over the other are doing so on their own aesthetic predilection. The stop should

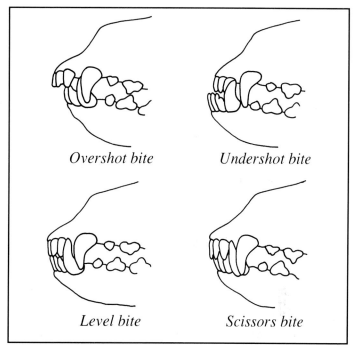

Overshot bite   Undershot bite

Level bite   Scissors bite

not be pronounced; neither absent nor too definite. There have always been myths surrounding this breed, and some are interesting, even though they may have no direct relevance. A Colonel Dickson wrote a book called *The Arab of the Desert*, and according to him: "The dog with two hair warts under the chin is better than one with only one, and the one having three or four such hair warts is very good."

The eye contributes greatly to the Saluki's expression, which should be dignified and gentle, with faithful, far-seeing eyes. In fact, the Saluki's eyesight is extraordinary, they can detect quarry long before the human eye can sight it. A Sheikh was once heard to remark:"My hawk has the eye of my Saluki." The colouring of the eyes should be dark to hazel. The interpretation of hazel causes some controversy among the fancy. This is understandable when you go to the dictionary for a definition. The *Collins Dictionary* describes hazel as a light yellowish-brown colour, while the *Oxford Dictionary* definition is reddish-brown or greenish-brown. There is also a degree of prejudice against the lighter-coloured eye. A light eye can look incongruous in a dark-coated hound, but the same colouring in a lighter dog might not attract the same criticism. In the chocolate-coloured Saluki, the lighter eye (sometimes called gooseberry) is correct. Round eyes are a fault, as are prominent, bulging and protruding eyes, which can be prone to injury. No mention is made of the third eyelid in the Breed Standard. This is a semi-cartilaginous structure, located at the inner corner of the eye. It is used as a protective device to shield the eye from injury, or to act as a windscreen wiper. Although our reasons are probably cosmetic, a black third eyelid does seem to gives a more harmonious expression to the eye.

The length of ear leathers is usually measured by pulling the ears forward to reach the corner of the mouth. The length of silky hair covering the ears varies enormously, depending on the breeding and coat of the exhibit. Some Salukis have feathering that drops well below the leathers, others have feathering that barely reaches this point. Neither should be penalised, for both meet the required standard. The smooth Saluki has no feathering on the ears. The use of the word 'mobile' in relation to the ears indicates that the ear should be capable of moving into various positions: lying close to the head when calm, and carried high when the dog is alert.

Teeth should have a scissor bite: one in which the outer surfaces of the lower teeth engage within the inner surfaces of the upper teeth when the mouth is shut. Overshot or undershot mouths must be regarded as a serious fault, a level bite is acceptable. The neck should be long, supple, well-muscled and set smoothly into the shoulders and withers. It should have great power and be very flexible, as this gives the Saluki the facility to reach downward and catch its quarry while galloping at great speed. A neck that is too long should be faulted, for it will be weaker in function.

FOREQUARTERS

A good front and rear assembly governs the dog's balance and gives it the ability to move freely. The action should be smooth and harmonious. The bone angles that most influence movement are the shoulder and hip joints, and their correct configuration is known as the angulation. Correct front and rear angulation provides an effortless stride and a smooth action; essential for a working sighthound. Insufficient angulation tends to shorten the stride, affects the gaiting pattern and makes the movement stilted and choppy. When the dog is moving, the front assembly acts as a shock-absorbing mechanism, taking the body weight and absorbing the impact from the ground as it counter-balances the drive from the rear. It performs four basic functions. Firstly, it absorbs impact; secondly, it supports about 60 per cent of the dog's body weight, leaving the hindquarters comparatively free to provide the energy and push from the rear; thirdly, the front endeavours to maintain balance while moving; and fourthly, the front assists the hindquarters in propelling the dog forward, adding an extra push from the backward position of each step.

Problems with movement usually arise when one part of the body has to compensate for lack of balance, injury, or weakness in another part. The importance of angulation to overall conformation has resulted in authorities of canine anatomy specifying or inferring a set of ideal measurements. The Saluki Breed Standard states that the shoulders should be "sloping and set well back, well-muscled without being coarse." In common with many other standards, this does not give the specific requirements of "set well back". There is a widely held belief in the show world that a 45 degree slope of the shoulder will give the maximum extension and reach of the forelimbs when gaiting. This theory

Salukis displaying good fronts. Good fill-in of chest, straight parallel forearms with gently sloping pastern.

emanates from early writings, and has been perpetuated throughout the years. The tendency to accept, without question, what appears and is continually repeated in print, has led to its broad acceptance. However, in recent years, two eminent writers on dog assembly and movement, Rachel Page Elliott and Curtis M. Brown, have completely demolished this sacred cow. Using cineradiography (moving X-rays) and systems of measurements, it has been found that no normal long-legged dog has a 45 degree shoulder layback. Radiographic studies show that dogs standing with their forelegs beneath them have an average blade-set of about 30 degrees, measured up the scapula ridge off a vertical plane. Brown found that the the desirable layback angle of the shoulder blade varied with the function of the dog: sighthounds measured about 10 degrees steeper than good trotting dogs, who averaged 30 degrees. Brown was evaluating both trotting and galloping dogs, whereas Rachel Page Elliott's conclusion was based on the average dog and did not differentiate between breed or function, and this accounts for their apparent conflict of opinion.

The argument for a well laid back shoulder is based on the premise that it gives a greater forward reach. Tests carried out on various dogs have established that whenever the front paw is behind the shoulder blade or a rear paw is behind the hip joint, the paws deliver a forward thrust and increases the speed of the dog. When the front paw is on the ground in front of the shoulder blade or the rear paw is in front of the hip joint, they are acting as a brake and slowing the dog down. This rather puts into question the belief that a long forward reach is desirable, since it can only increase the braking force.

The shoulder or scapula is a long bone attached to the rib cage by muscle, not by bone joints. Muscles impart movement to the limbs; bones on their own are passive, requiring muscles to move them. However, muscles can only pull; they cannot push. This means that there must be a minimum of two muscles to move a bone: at least one to pull it in one direction and at least one to pull it in another. The major muscles that pull the front leg forward are attached to the

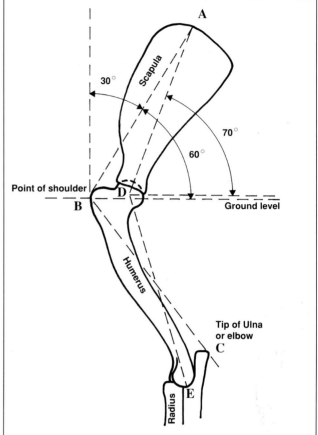

In the show ring, most judges measure the layback of shoulder by placing a fingers at points A and B, and estimate the angle created, either off the vertical or horizontal planes. Return and length of upper arm (humerus) is measured from points B and C. A more exact method is to measure A, D and E. This is the method used by Curtis M. Brown for his calculations.

shoulder blade and upper arm, and the main ones that pull the front leg towards the rear are fixed to the humerus. The humerus or upper arm slopes down and back to the elbow and should counter-balance the angle of the shoulder blade; it is normally longer than the scapula. A straight or over-angulated upper arm will throw the front assembly out of balance and therefore affect movement.

In the show ring, the usual way of evaluating the angles and length of bones in the front assembly is to place one finger at the top of the scapula (A), another on the point of shoulder (B), and then move the top finger down to the tip of the elbow (C).

Angles can be calculated off either the horizontal or vertical planes. It should be emphasised that measurements taken in this way are only approximate. A more realistic method of determining actual bone placement is to trace the spine of the scapula (A-D) and then continue to the bottom of the humerus (E). The two systems of measurement differ by between five to ten degrees. So when Curtis M. Brown advocates that a shoulder angle of about 20 degrees in a Saluki is correct for the function of the dog, when using the first measurement system, these angles could well be evaluated in the show ring as between 25 and 30 degrees. There should be sufficient separation between the two shoulder blades when the dog is standing normally. If there is too little space, then, as the dog lowers its head, the blades slide together, and when they touch one another the dog is unable to lower its head any further. This is obviously a problem in a hunting breed.

The front legs, whether viewed from the front or side, should be straight and long from the elbow to the wrist (pastern joint), and in proportion to the body. The Arabs say that it should be difficult to press the elbows together: this is to test springiness, development and strength of the muscles which draw the elbows against the chest. For galloping dogs, "out at the elbow" is a defect, usually caused by the

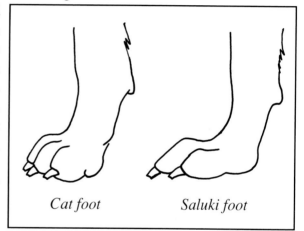

Cat foot   *Saluki foot*

shoulder blade being set too far forward: it often causes "toeing in." Conversely, "tied at the elbows" is equally undesirable. It severely restricts front movement and causes the front legs to swing forward in an outward arc, which is known as "paddling". In the Saluki, the length of leg from the bottom of the brisket to the ground is slightly longer than the distance from the bottom of the brisket to the top of the withers. The height of the Saluki, measured from the top of the withers to the ground, allows for an astonishing variation in size of five inches, unparalleled in other breeds. It was this point which caused the biggest controversy when the original standard was drawn up in 1923. On one side stood Brigadier General Lance with his taller dogs, on the other side was the Hon. Florence Amherst with the smaller type. Eventually a compromise was reached and the standard defined as "should average 23 to 28 inches at the shoulder, bitches proportionally smaller".

Bone should be bladed or oval, but remember, heavy bone is not necessarily synonymous with quality. Round bone does not lend itself to speed and is mentioned in the standard as a fault. The front pasterns should be strong with a slight forward slant from the wrist to the foot. They are the shock-absorbers of the front assembly, designed to absorb the impact of the paw with the ground and lessen it so the shoulders do not receive undue shock. When galloping, at the set-down point of the paw, the pastern joint is bent with the initial impact. By the time the paw is directly under the shoulder blade, the pastern is bent about 90 degrees forward and the stop pad is on the ground. This forward bending of the pastern stretches the tendons and stores energy. As the paw extends further back, the pastern joint is straightened and the energy is released to propel the dog forward.

Another distinctive feature of the Saluki is its feet: they are quite different from the feet of other sighthounds. They should be of moderate length and well-arched. They should not be splayed out, but at the same time they should not appear cat-footed. They should be strong and supple with feathering between the toes (except in the smooth). The two inner toes on each foot are longer than the two outer toes. The front feet, when viewed from the front, may point outward at a very slight angle when standing. The pads should be thick and springy. This, coupled with the length of the foot, enables the hounds to traverse long distances on both sand and rough terrain. The best way to examine the thickness of pads is to lift the front foot towards the rear, horse-fashion, as this is more comfortable for the dog. The front paws are larger in area than the rear paws. As a comparison, the hare foot is similar in proportion to the Saluki foot, but narrower and not so long. The cat foot is smaller in proportion, short-toed and almost round.

THE BODY ASSEMBLY

The topline is one of the most salient characteristics of the Saluki, differing from all other sighthounds. The back should be fairly broad, with the muscles slightly arched over the loin, but not roached. The loin, because of the muscles, is very lightly rounded. The hip bones should be prominent and sufficiently wide apart, and the croup falls away slightly. In *Hutchinson's Dog Encyclopedia* it is stated that the Arabs emphasised prominent hip bones as a desirable quality, looking for enough space to place three or four fingers between the hip bones. A deep hollow between the bones was considered an asset. Another source of Arabian writings states: "The main slope of the body should be from the tail to shoulder, giving an impression of speed, the hindquarters being higher than the shoulders." Saluki handlers should be careful not to pull the hindquarters too far back to emphasise angulation or to cover more ground. This can either flatten the topline or make it fall away, destroying a distinguishing feature of the breed. Mrs Hope Waters, of the famous Burydown

A balanced Saluki with well-proportioned head, moderate stop, long neck flowing into withers, good topline with a nice arch overt the loin, beautiful croup and set-on tail, strong 1st and 2nd thighs with rear angulation that shows no exaggerations.

kennels, reiterated the words of a revered judge of yesteryear, when she said "The Saluki's outline should fit into a matchbox standing on its side." Without entering into any debate as to whether it was a "Swan Vesta" or a "Bryant May", the principle was, and still is, that the body length should not be too long – body length refers to the distance from the forechest to the point of buttock. Curtis Brown advocates that a squarer body shape is more functional for a breed designed for galloping and endurance. Apparently, the first thing that an Arab looks for in a Saluki is a deep and strong chest. The Breed Standard replaces the word "strong" with "moderately narrow". Looking at a fully matured Saluki from the side, the brisket should almost reach the point of elbow. Judges beware: a clever handler will disguise a shallow brisket by brushing up the elbow feathering. Viewed from the front, there should be a good fill-in of forechest, with about a hand's-width of space between the two forelegs. The dreaded inverted "V" front (lack of fill-in) is a fault, although allowances should be made for younger stock. Looking from above the dog, there should be a clearly defined curving out of the ribs from behind the withers to the front of the loin. The ribs have two major functions: firstly to provide protection for the lungs and heart-space; secondly to aid breathing. An adequate length of rib cage is therefore desirable. The Arabs looked for a narrow, strong and well-muscled loin, one that a man should be able to close his two hands around. In fact, loin straps (leather straps wrapped around the loin) were sometimes used by the Arabs to maintain this feature.

The coat pattern is another individual feature of the breed. It is short-haired, except for the feathering, with a soft silky texture. However, it is difficult for the judge to evaluate this aspect, as modern shampoos and conditioners can work wonders even on a bad coat. The current Breed Standard states that feathering on the throat is "permissible, but not desirable". As far as we are concerned, this is an astonishing statement, for this feathering is a most attractive feature and another individual characteristic of the breed. Admittedly, it can make a neck look too thick; but if that is the case, a bit of pruning will solve the problem Although specific colours are mentioned within the Breed Standard, both British breed clubs have jointly submitted proposals to the Kennel Club to amend this to encompass all colours. If this is approved, it will allow the colour brindle, which was previously excluded. The brindle colouring has been a hotly debated point within the breed. At present, there are no Salukis in this country with this colouring, although several have been reported in the Middle East and Europe.

HINDQUARTERS

The main driving force responsible for producing movement in the dog is the hindquarters. The combination of pelvic and upper thigh muscles give speed, while endurance and staying power is provided by the lower thighs and rear pasterns. The front assembly supports and assists movement by providing a stabilising and supportive role, but it plays only a small part in producing propulsion. The croup is a muscular area between the loin and the tail and overlays the pelvis from the hip joints to the buttocks. The pelvic girdle is firmly attached to both sides of the sacral vertebrae of the spinal column and slopes downwards from this point towards the rear at an angle of approximately thirty degrees. The hip socket lies more or less halfway between the spinal joint and the pelvic tuber, and the head of the femur or thigh bone, the longest single bone in the dog's anatomy, fits into this. The femur runs downwards and forward to meet the tibia and fibula at the stifle joint. The muscles that surround the femur are the thigh muscles. These should be well-developed, and when viewed from the side, they should show good width. A thirty degree slope of the pelvis facilitates a good rear extension of the hind legs for propulsion, and it also allows the legs to be carried sufficiently forward under the body. A flatter pelvic angle gives a greater rear extension, but too short a front stride; whereas a steeper pelvis will shorten the rearward extension and give a more stilted action.

The angle formed at the stifle joint by the femur with the junction of the tibia/fibula determines stifle angulation – and in the Saluki this should be moderate. The tibia and fibula together form the lower thigh, which slopes rearwards towards the hocks. The tibia bone is located in the front of the lower thigh and is far larger than the fibula, which is at the rear. Both are fixed together at the top and bottom ends, making them into a single leverage unit. The lower thigh is covered in muscle known as the second thigh, and this should be well-muscled. R. H. Smythe writes in his book *Conformation of the Dog*: "Practically the whole propelling force of the hind limb is dependent on the ability of the dog to straighten the leg from the state of angulation to complete extension, as forcibly and rapidly as may be required. This is dependent entirely upon the muscle power of a well-developed second thigh."

When Salukis are posed in the show position, the rear pastern should be placed at ninety degrees to the ground. The tip of the paw should align vertically under the rearmost point of the pelvis. If the paw is further back than this when the rear pastern is vertical, then the dog has excessive rear angulation. Sickle hocks are present if the tip of the paw is placed under the pelvis and the rear pastern slopes backwards. A straight hock is caused by insufficient angulation between the lower thigh and the rear pastern. Cow hocks are when both hocks turn in towards each other, when the dog is viewed from the rear. Conversely, hocks that point outward are called bow or barrel-hocked. We are often told in canine publications that front and rear angulations should be balanced. This implies that both front and rear angles should be similar: i.e. the shoulder angle should roughly equate to the femur angle and the humerus angle should be comparable to the tibia angle. Curtis Brown is of the opinion that in dogs designed for the gallop, the front angles should be steeper than those of the rear. He concludes that dog fanciers tend to put everything into a "universal standard" based upon what produces an ideal trotting style, without paying due regard to the different functions of each breed. The Saluki is a galloping dog with great powers of endurance therefore its trotting style should not be compared with dogs that have been bred for different purposes.

The tail is the final portion of the spine. The point where the tail joins the croup is called the set-on. The set-on should be low, i.e. below the topline and at the base of the croup. Primarily for aesthetic reasons, we like to see a curved croup from the hip bones to the tail set, with the set-on showing no demarcation lines. However, it should be pointed out that in very hot weather the Saluki tends to lift its tail slightly to let some air circulate and provide natural air conditioning, and allowances should be made for this when judging. The tail is carried naturally in a curve; it is well-feathered on the underside with long silky hair, but it should not be bushy. The length of tail is important, as the Saluki uses his tail as a rudder when running at speed. To measure the length of tail either pull the tail downwards, the tip of the tail bone should reach approximately to the hocks; or pull the tail down and under the rear legs and up around the loin, the tip of the tail should reach a point midway between the two hip bones. The tail is also a good barometer for ascertaining the mood of the Saluki. If the tail is held tight under its body, it is either miserable or nervous; if it hangs naturally down with a slight natural curve, it is relaxed; when the tail is carried high the dog is probably in high spirits. In the show ring when the dog is stacked, the tail is normally tucked under the body in an "S" shape or hangs loosely in a curve. When the dog is moving, the tail extends to create a smooth, picturesque, free-flowing outline, with the tail just below the topline. Younger stock sometimes carry their tails high (gay), and this should not be penalised.

MOVEMENT

Perhaps the most controversial points in the 1986 Breed Standard are under the heading of movement. The phases used to describe the gait of the Saluki are contradictory in their interpretation. For example, the description "light, lifting and effortless" cannot equate with "long flat strides". If a dog moves with long flat strides, how can they, at the same time, be light and lifting? Similarly, how can a dog displaying both reach and drive move effortlessly? The wording of the revised standard, agreed at the Special General Meeting of both breed clubs, states: "At the trot: appearing effortless, light, smooth, lifting and flowing. No hackneyed action or plodding. Unexaggerated. Viewed from the front or rear, movement should reveal a natural tendency for the limbs to converge towards a central line of travel, with no side-stepping, crossing or interfering. Should be balanced." This, we believe, is a much better description of a Saluki's movement.

Many people have tried to describe the typical movement of the Saluki at the trot. The Hon. Florence Amherst (Amherstia) described the Saluki's gait as neat, dainty and prancing, with no hackneyed action or plodding. Miss Amherst also wrote in *Hutchinson's Dog Encyclopedia*: "The action of the Saluki is different from that of a Greyhound. It is more springy when walking, and at a trot it is more prancing, which is a striking point." Mrs H. M. Parkhouse (Shammar), in a critique after judging at Blackpool in 1958 stated that the poor movement seen in most of the entries was not typical. "I have thought for some time that we are in danger of losing the true Saluki

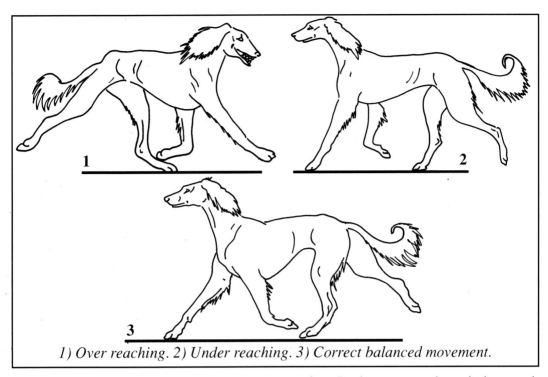

1) Over reaching. 2) Under reaching. 3) Correct balanced movement.

action, which should be lighter and more prancing. In the pre-war days, judges took more notice of movement than they do today, and unless a hound moved with the correct dainty, prancing action it would not get very far in the award list." Another judge's show report from yesteryear said: "Are we losing sight of what constitutes typical breed movement? By this I mean that particular freedom of movement combined with extreme lightness and utter grace. Our breed should not be plodders."

The major problem in defining a criterion for movement is that in the show ring we are looking for a balanced dog that moves correctly and smoothly at the trot. The dog world has agreed on the correct structure for an ideal trotting dog, but it has forgotten the original purpose of each breed: not all dogs were created for this function. The trot of the Saluki should be based on a style of movement that is both economic and energy-conserving; using excessive energy at a slow gait is wasteful and inefficient. We must never forget that the Saluki was bred to be a galloping dog with a high endurance capability and its trotting style should reflect this aspect.

Rachel Page Elliott has, in our opinion, prepared an excellent description of Saluki movement: "The Saluki falls into the category of hounds built for great speed at the gallop, but at the show ring he must be judged at the trot. Though the trot does not reveal the boldness in the hunt, it does tell us much about his skeletal structure and physical condition. At this gait I look for lightness of movement with a proud

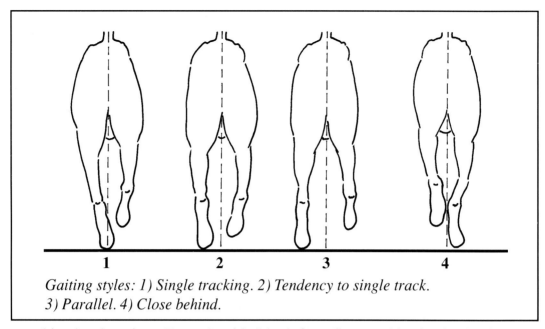

Gaiting styles: 1) Single tracking. 2) Tendency to single track.
3) Parallel. 4) Close behind.

searching head carriage. From the side I look for a firm working back with freedom in the shoulders and smooth opening of the shoulder joints. Rear action should be rhythmic and effortless, with no over-reaching or side-stepping. The gait should have a spring without stiltedness, fluidity without extreme effort. Coming and going, the limbs from the shoulders and hips to the pads, should swing without twisting as they fold and extend, even as they reach inward towards the central support beneath the body. Call it single tracking, the tendency to single track, or convergence, as you will – but not parallel tracking, because nature did not so design a Saluki."

There has always been a strong divergence of opinion, held by leading breeders, regarding parallel movement versus single tracking. We were surprised, and delighted, that the wording advocating the latter was unanimously adopted at the Special General Meeting without any disagreement. Perhaps some of the misunderstanding has arisen because in the standing position, the dog's legs are parallel, and they also seem to be parallel as they start to walk, but as the dog starts to move faster the natural tendency is for the dog's legs to converge. When the dog breaks into a trot, his body is supported by only two legs at a time, the two feet diagonally opposite each other striking the ground together in an alternating sequence, front right with rear left, then front left with rear right. The dog now relies on forward momentum to retain balance, usually over a central column of support, in order to travel easily and efficiently. Parallel movement, when either viewed from the front or the rear, is when both the front and rear legs move alternately in a straight line to each other. Dogs that move parallel, when trotting, may be doing so because of restricted shoulders or elbow joints, steep and short upper arms, or other reasons.

Single tracking, or convergence, is when both the front and rear legs converge towards a single line. The legs travel straight from the shoulder and hip joint to the pads without interfering or crossing each other. Convergence should never be confused with "moving too close". Moving close is a fault caused by either the front or hind limbs being insufficiently separated from one another during movement, and in extreme cases interfering with or crossing each other. Salukis have a tendency to pace when walking: i.e. both the front and rear legs on either side of the body move back and forth as a pair, causing a rolling or rocking motion of the dog's body similar to a camel's gait. This movement is characteristic of some long-legged breeds and is used to conserve energy over a long distance at slow speeds. In the show ring it is frowned upon. To avoid pacing, handlers usually start by moving their dogs away quickly, and at the same time giving a quick jerk of the lead.

Judges can discover a lot from observing a dog moving in the show ring, as a dog will not move correctly if it is not balanced throughout. Structural faults of a posed dog can be disguised by an experienced handler, skilled in the art of concealing bad points and emphasising the virtues. But on the move, a perceptive judge can evaluate overall balance, body length/leg ratio, head carriage and proportion of head to neck, shoulder and hip angulation, topline and arch over the loin, tail set and carriage, length of stride, front and rear movement, soundness and muscle condition. However, sometimes even a well-constructed dog can move badly. This can usually be attributed to one of several factors: poor condition and lack of muscle tone from insuffient exercise; excessive weight; ring shyness or nervousness, which in extreme cases cause some Salukis to lower their heads and crouch around the ring when moving.

All the points relating to the Breed Standard discussed within this chapter apply equally to the smooth Saluki, with the exception of the coat, which has no feathering. Judging and evaluating the qualities, conformation and aesthetics of this exquisite breed is a continuous learning process; in the words of Ernest Hemingway: "There are some things in life that cannot be learned quickly, and time, which is all we have, must be paid heavily for their acquiring."

Multi-Ch. Abrisa vom Felsenkeller (Samoens Sakbar Walad ex Saliha Durrani) bred by C. Hess and owned by Tim Teillers. "Breeze" was Best in Show at the World Winners Show two years running, 1985 and 1986.

Chapter Seven

IN THE SHOW RING

Showing is great fun, and it is not as complicated as it may at first appear. Equally, "dog people" are neither bizarre nor eccentric, and you will discover that the sport of showing dogs is one of the most sociable and pleasurable hobbies you could hope to discover. Once bitten with the "bug" you will join the hundreds of other people who travel mile upon mile, every week, to satisfy their addiction. Most first-time Saluki owners never see this as a raison d'etre, but you will be surprised how many, sooner or later, get gripped with show fever. The euphoria of the win, the disappointment of losing, new-found friends, the spectacle, all contribute to a great day out.

Like most people, we purchased our first Saluki, Jazirat Bey Sadi ("Abi"), as a pet, with no intention of showing. She was a lovely cream bitch, who totally captivated us with her ethereal charm, aristocratic demeanour and beauty. Mrs Hope Waters (Burydown) was later to comment in a judging critique: "...cream of the highest quality, just like a piece of Dresden china...". Whether it was out of curiosity, naivete, or arrogance, we decided to share her beauty in the show ring with others. We were convinced that all we had to do was to enter the ring and the red cards (first prizes) would be showered upon us like confetti. Not so! There is much more to showing a dog than putting a collar and lead around its neck and running round the ring a couple of times. We learnt the hard way, countless disappointments, post mortems – "the judge must have been blind," and other similar platitudes. However, we did have our share of successes, and the thrill when she won her first Challenge Certificate was indescribable, and certainly worth all the previous heartaches. Apart from the thrill of winning, there is also a real camaraderie between fellow exhibitors, together with an atmosphere of excitement and friendly competition. We have made countless friends, both in the UK and throughout the world, as a result of our involvement with Salukis. There is no other sport or hobby where hospitality is given unquestionably by fellow competitors. Perhaps Saluki owners have unwittingly inherited the Bedouin's rules of cordiality, where all guests are welcome and receive the best hospitality the host can offer. To the newcomer, the whole procedure of dog shows must seem esoteric and bemusing, but don't get discouraged. It really doesn't take very long to grasp the principles involved. If you embark on serious showing, you will enjoy yourself all the more if you do not get too down-hearted about a string of poor results – the good times are all the better for the bad times. Always remember, the best Saluki is the one that you take home after the show, even if the judge didn't agree.

When you have entered for a show, don't forget to put the date into your

Ch. Baazighah du Ja'arid, Norway's Saluki of the Year 1987. Owned and bred by Livar and Malmfrid Dubland.

diary. That might seem obvious, but you will be surprised how many seasoned exhibitors have turned up on the wrong day. Also check the schedule for the specified time that dogs have to arrive by, and note the time judging is expected to commence. Arriving a day late is annoying, but it's just as frustrating to arrive on the correct day only to discover that the class you have entered has already been judged. When you have made the decision to compete, you need to prepare yourself and your Saluki for the big day. Your local canine society will probably have weekly training classes for handling. These can be both educational and good fun. They give a sound grounding, building up your confidence and familiarising both yourself and your dog with ring procedure. Your puppy will also learn to socialise with other breeds of dogs. Showing a dog to its best advantage takes a lot of skill, which is not at first obvious to the casual observer. Practice makes perfect, and the more experience you get, the better you will be. A skilled handler hides the dog's faults and emphasises its good points. The aim, primarily, is to accentuate your dog's virtues and conceal any imperfections from the judge, who only has a limited time to examine each entry. You can practise your handling technique at home. The best way to learn to stack (stand) your dog in the show position is by using a mirror. If you don't have a full length mirror in a convenient location, simply lean a mirror against a suitable wall. The mirror will enable you to see if your Saluki is over-stretched at the rear, or rocking at the front, or any other faults. When you are handling the dog, don't pick it up under its belly. This causes the dog to roach its back and spoils the topline. Keep a check on your use of the lead: it looks tidier if the spare length is folded up into the palm of your hand; it is unsightly if it is allowed to dangle. Try to accomplish the stance with a minimum of fuss. Over-handling can make the dog nervous and distract the judge.

The garden is the best place to practise movement. It is useful if your partner or a friend pretends to be the judge: they will be able to assess the best speed to gait your dog. All dogs have an ideal trotting speed. If you move the dog too fast or too slowly it can significantly affect the gait. Most Salukis move best on a loose lead, held in the left hand, with the handler about one or two paces in front of the dog. Try to move away smoothly and in a straight line. Try not to jerk the lead, as this only throws the dog off balance and disturbs its gait. Practise moving both in a triangular pattern and straight up and down. When you reach the turning point on the up-and-down exercise, slow down and allow the dog to move around you in a clockwise semi-circle without significantly decreasing its speed. Remember, practice makes perfect.

You will also need to purchase a few items of equipment – the range can be added to at a later date as you become more familiar with your own requirements. You will need grooming equipment – combs, brushes, and nail-clippers; a blanket for the dog's bed; a towel – if the day is very warm it can be dampened and placed over the dog in the ring to keep it cool, and if the ground is muddy you can use it to clean up your dog; drinking bowl; benching chain; and a show lead. Most Salukis are shown with a light nylon lead. There are numerous varieties and colours available. We always choose a colour similar to the dog that we are showing. Your local petshop will probably have a few show leads on view, but the best range can be seen at the trade stands which form a major part of every dog show.

When the day dawns, arrive in good time and make your way to your numbered bench. All Championship Shows are benched and the show secretary of the organising Canine Society will have confirmed your entry and enclosed an exhibit number, which corresponds to your benching number. Most other shows are unbenched and your entry is usually unconfirmed. Settle your dog down on the bench, with a blanket to make it comfortable, and secure it with a benching chain to the point provided. Make sure you have a bowl of fresh drinking water available – we usually carry our water in a thermos flask for convenience. We also take along titbits of either cooked sausages or liver. These can be useful as bait in the ring; it helps to attract your dog's attention and keeps it alert. Don't forget that the dog is the star, and like all stars it should be pampered. The dog's performance in the ring must be flawless, and it is up to you to ensure that it is relaxed, and in the proper frame of mind to give its best. We usually keep our dogs calm and on the benches until the class before ours is being judged. Then we lightly groom each dog, giving a brush over their coat and combing all the feathering. This is all you need to do, as the dog should have been thoroughly groomed the previous evening. We then take the dogs for a warm-up session, and we give them an opportunity to perform any toilet requirements. However, make sure you dispose of any excreta, as it is against Kennel Club rules to leave a mess lying in the showground.

When entering the ring, your dog should appear confident and familiar with the handling, stance and movements required. This is the time to put into practice all that you have learnt at training classes. The ring-presence of your dog has a lot to do with its success. If you are nervous or lacking in confidence, this is transmitted down the lead to your dog, and the dog will mirror your feelings and probably give a lacklustre performance. It is a good idea to wear clothes that compliment the colour of your dog. For example: don't wear black trousers or a black dress if you are showing a black dog – the dog's outline will be lost when it is viewed by the judge.

To begin with, all competing dogs will line up in the show stance, side by side, along one side of the ring, so that the judge can get an overall impression. The class will then be asked to trot around the ring together. This gives the dogs a chance to

"Once around the ring please".   *FALAPA, August 1989.*

relax and the judge will be able to compare side movement and overall balance. Each dog is then individually presented to the judge, who will go over the exhibit, checking its head for balance, the occiput, stop, ear placement, colour and shape of eyes, teeth and bite. The length of neck will be assessed, the shoulder for width and layback; the topline, the shape of ribs for depth, length and spring. The judge will look at front angulation, the fill-in of chest; feet; rear angulation; croup; upper and lower thighs, and length of tail. If the dog is a male he will check that it is entire. Then you will be requested to move with your dog, first in a triangular shape and then up and down in a straight line. This gives the judge the opportunity to assess movement and general bearing. After each exhibit has been seen, the whole class will line up again, side by side, for the judge to select his placements. The judge's decisions are a matter of personal opinion, and opinions vary between different judges, although all are judging to the same Breed Standard. It is this element of personal interpretation that enables dog shows to survive; if every judge was in accord with every other, there would only ever be one winner.

All shows in the UK are held under the jurisdiction of the Kennel Club, who define the rules and regulations governing all pedigree dog shows. There are several different types of dog shows with conformation classes:

Sanction Show: These are restricted to members of the club organising the show, and only members are permitted to exhibit. A show confined to one breed must not include more than ten classes and a show with more than one breed no more than twenty-five classes.

Limited Show: Like the sanction show, entry is restricted to members of the organising society. Dogs who have won Challenge Certificates are not allowed to compete. Both the sanction and limited shows are often used by exhibitors to give their new dogs ring experience.

Open Shows: These shows are open to all exhibitors and are usually unbenched. Quite often they are held in conjunction with an agricultural or county show, which helps to turn the day into a family occasion.

Championship Shows: These shows are also open to all exhibitors, although some are specifically confined to breed clubs. For example, the Saluki or Gazelle Hound Club and the Northern Saluki Club each hold Championship Shows. The main difference between an Open Show and a Championship Show is that the Kennel Club Challenge Certificate is awarded at the latter.

There are about twenty-nine Championship shows with Saluki classes scheduled in Britain each year, starting in January with Crufts. Saluki entries vary from show to show, depending usually on the judge and the geographic location. Classes are separated into dogs and bitches, then further divided into age and achievement groups such as: Puppy, Junior, Novice, Post Graduate, Limit and Open. Full details regarding entry requirements for the classes are published in each schedule. Each class is judged, one at a time, the dogs first and then the bitches. From each class the judge will choose and place five dogs: first, second, third, reserve and very highly commended. On completion of all the classes, the judge will ask to see the class winners again (so long as they didn't enter a subsequent class and get beaten). From the "unbeaten dogs" he will select his choice of best dog, and award it with the Kennel Club Challenge Certificate (CC, also referred to as "the ticket"). The dog considered the second best is awarded the Reserve Challenge Certificate (RCC). This award can be presented to the second placed dog in the class won by the CC winner, or any of the remaining unbeaten dogs. The Saluki is a slow-maturing dog, and so it is rare for top honours to be given to a puppy. The whole procedure is then repeated for the bitches, with another CC and RCC winner being selected. The judge now has to select Best of Breed (BOB) – chosen from both the CC winners. The

Mrs Hope Waters judging at Santa Barbara, 1988.

Best of Breed winner continues into the Hound Group to compete against other Hound Best of Breed winners. The winner of this Group competes with the winners from the Gundog, Terrier, Toy, Working and Utility Groups, and one of these six dogs will be awarded Best in Show; the runner-up will be Reserve Best in Show.

Although success in the Best in Show and Group Rings is much sought after, the Challenge Certificate is the prime objective of each exhibitor and the subsequent "making-up" of their dog to a Champion. To become a Champion, a dog has to obtain three CCs from three different judges. Competition for these "tickets" is intense, and as a result, they are very difficult to obtain. Under the British system, the CC is competed for by all the dogs entered within the breed at each show, both Champions and non-Champions. Throughout the rest of the World, CCs or their equivalent are competed for with the Champions excluded. The Champions only compete for Best of Breed or Best Opposite Sex. In the USA, the governing body is the American Kennel Club (AKC), which controls all rules and regulations governing dog shows. The equivalent shows to the British Championship shows are the Speciality (one breed) and All-Breed Shows. To become a Champion each dog must obtain fifteen points. Points are awarded, from one to five, at each show, depending upon the number of dogs competing. The fifteen points required must be won under at least three different judges; among these fifteen points two must be of three or more points (majors) won under two different judges. There are usually five classes in which dogs accumulating points towards their Championship can compete: Puppy (these are frequently sub-divided by age into two classes – six to nine months, and nine to twelve months), Novice, Bred by Exhibitor, American-bred and Open. After these classes have been judged, first-place winners compete against each other in the winners class (unbeaten dogs). The dog selected is the Winners Dog, who receives the Championship points allocated for the show. The same process is repeated for the bitches, until a Winners Bitch is selected. It is only the Winners Dog and Bitch that receive the Championship points. Both the Winners Dog and Winners Bitch then move forward into the Best of Breed class, and there they are joined by all the recorded Champions that have been entered. When this class has been assessed, the judge will choose the Best of Breed (BOB). A Best of Winners is also selected from either the Winners Dog or the Winners Bitch, and a Best of Opposite Sex. If either the Winners Dog or Winners Bitch is awarded Best of Breed, then he or she will automatically become Best of Winners. The Best of Breed winner will compete in the Hound Group, and if successful, will contend for Best in Show.

Throughout Europe, each country has its own national equivalent of the Kennel Club, but they are governed by regulations laid down by the FCI – the Federation Cynologique International. At FCI shows, each judge has to write a critique on every exhibit; this is written on the spot and handed to the exhibitor during the show. The judge also has to grade each dog: excellent, very good, good or sufficient. Judging by this method, obviously takes much longer and is, in our opinion, not as exciting for the spectators, as the continuity is constantly being broken. Two shows which annually attract very large Saluki entries in Europe and Scandinavia are the Club Francais des Amateurs de Levriers D'asie, Persans et Afghans (FALAPA), held in France, and Skokloster's Saluki Club Show in Sweden. Both are well worth a visit and attract a big crowd of international spectators.

Chapter Eight

THE OBEDIENCE TRAIL

There are many misconceptions among dog people, regarding the Saluki's capability for obedience training. Handlers working with the preferred breeds, such as Labrador Retrievers, German Shepherd Dogs and Border Collies, often comment that the Saluki is unable to adapt to the disciplines required in the obedience ring. Salukiphiles, romancing about the noble companion of the Bedouin, think the Saluki is aloof, and above such trivial pursuits. Neither of these suppositions is based on fact, but both views have an element of truth. It's all really a matter of what obedience means to you, and what you expect to accomplish by training your dog.

The majority of owners simply require a well-behaved dog, which is under control when it is out of doors. There is, however, a hard core of enthusiasts who want to compete and win in obedience competitions. If winning is your prime objective, then the Saluki is not the ideal choice of dog. Salukis are highly intelligent, independent, aloof, and they excel at chasing quarry over great distances – the job they were bred to do. In contrast, the herding and working breeds have been bred to work in close co-operation with their masters and to obey their commands. Does this mean that Salukis cannot or should not compete in trials? Again, the answer lies in what you are hoping to achieve. You don't have to get a rosette or a ribbon to be successful.

A Saluki competing in an obedience trial.   *Gerald Holly*

The challenge is to build and develop your relationship with your dog, and the reward is knowing both of you have performed the disciplines to the best of your mutual ability.

Obedience trials are a sport, and all participants should be guided by the principles of good sportsmanship. The object of the trials is to demonstrate the usefulness of the dog as a companion of people, and not merely to display the dog's ability to follow specific routines in the obedience ring. The contestants are required to perform the same exercise in substantially the same way, in order that the relative quality of each performance may be scored and compared, but the underlying aim is to produce dogs that have been trained and conditioned to behave in the home, in public places, and in the presence of other dogs. Training takes a great deal of time, patience and dedication. The Saluki's character does not always adapt easily to the rigours of ring obedience, but the experience will never be dull, and the fulfilment of competing in your first trial will repay all your hard work.

In Britain, very few Saluki owners venture into competitive obedience trials. In

Ch. Timaru Tanqueray CD CC (Ch. Timaru Zinfadel CDX ex Ch. Ismahane marantthe CD). Bred and owned by John and Lesley Brabyn, Mill Valley, California, Tanqueray combines outstanding American and English bloodlines in her pedigree. She is the only Saluki in recent times to hold titles in the open field, show and obedience rings.

America and Canada there is a far greater interest and participation in the sport, with many Salukis winning obedience titles. In North America, obedience judging is based on the dog's and handler's ability to perform a series of prescribed exercises. Each exercise has a number of points allocated to it. The dog/handler team commence with 200 points, and points are deducted for each error noted by the judge. The team has to achieve a minimum of 170 points as a qualifying score, and they must receive more than 50 per cent of the allotted points awarded for each exercise.

The American Kennel Club recognizes three obedience titles, and after each title has been awarded, the appropriate letters are added to the dog's name. In order of ascending difficulty, the titles are: Companion Dog (CD), Companion Dog Excellent (CDX) and Utility Dog (UD). Each title requires three qualifying scores under three different judges, and each title must be won in the ascending order of merit. The first title in obedience is the CD, which is awarded from the Novice Classes. The exercises performed are: heel on leash including a figure eight pattern, stand for examination (handler six feet away from dog), heel free, recall (come when called by the handler who is about thirty feet away), long sit (for one minute with handler across the ring) and long down (for three minutes with handler across the ring). After a dog wins its CD, it moves on to compete for the CDX title. This is earned from the Open Classes, and as you would expect, it involves more complicated exercises, all performed off the leash. In addition to the exercises in the Novice classes, the dog must: drop on recall, retrieve on a flat surface, retrieve over a high jump (equivalent to one and a quarter times the height of the dog at its withers) and a broad jump (twice the width of the high jump). The long sit and the long down are for three and five minutes respectively, with the handler completely out of sight. The exercises for the more difficult UD title are: signal exercise, scent discrimination of two different articles – one of a rigid metal, the other of leather; directed retrieve; moving stand and examination; and directed jumping. The American Kennel Club publishes a pamphlet entitled *Obedience Regulations* which is very informative and explains in detail what is required for each class, and the number of points allocated to the various exercises.

Chapter Nine

COURSING IN BRITAIN AND AMERICA

Since time immemorial, man has used dogs to hunt down and catch game to provide food for his family. Sighthounds – dogs that pursue their quarry by sight rather than by scent – originated in what we now call the Middle East. The Saluki was the hunting hound of the Bedouin Arab, and was one of his most treasured possessions. The Saluki's sight, speed and endurance made it an efficient and lethal hunter, and therefore the breed was kept pure, in order to retain these outstanding qualities. The result, is one of the most beautiful breeds of pedigree dogs that exist today.

In the 1951 Saluki or Gazelle Hound Club Handbook, the Saluki's special abilities are summed up as: "A capable hound of the chase, with sloping shoulders, racy hindquarters, flexible loin, deep ribs, long-stretching limbs and muscular neck, he is admirably adapted for the work to which he has been bred for so many centuries – the hunting of gazelle and hare as a meat supply for his master. He is fashioned for speed, quick turning – running on rough ground and for endurance."

An early coursing meeting held at Cleve Farm, Minster, Thanet in 1933. Mrs Cleeve, on horseback, donated the prestigious Cleve Cup which is still competed for, and it is one of the premier events in the coursing calender each season.

The meet at Cleve Farm in 1933.

COURSING IN GREAT BRITAIN

It was in order to preserve the hunting skills of the Saluki that organised coursing was started in England in 1925, masterminded by Brigadier and Mrs Lance. The first recorded meeting was held near Chipping Norton, Oxfordshire, and The Shipton Stakes was divided between Mrs G. M. Lance's Sarona Nada and Mrs F. Mitchell's Egyptian Bey. In 1927, Miss Sybil Kerrison was appointed honorary secretary of the Saluki Coursing Club, a position which she held until she resigned in 1934. Then, as now, the main objective of the club was to preserve the hunting instincts of the breed, rather than let it become exclusively a show specimen. All serious Saluki breeders are committed to producing a dog that is true to the type that has been inherited through the centuries, and one that is capable of performing its original function.

From 1934 until the outbreak of the second World War, Commander B.S.M. Adams R.N., of the well-known Haredam prefix, was the club secretary, and he organised all the coursing events. Haredam were one of the most successful coursing kennels of this era, producing two outstanding dogs – Haredam Viking, a white dog, and his white daughter, Knightellington Haredam Calliope, owned by Lady Gardener (Knightellington). The dam of Calliope was Haredam Princess Jean, and her pedigree lists two sires: Haredam Viking and his litter brother Haredam Crusader. Both the dam and the sires emanated from the renowned Ch. Sarona Kelb. In fact, both dogs mated Princess Jean, and either could have been the father, but the majority thought of her as the daughter of Viking. During Calliope's illustrious coursing career, she won the coveted Cleve Cup three times, a feat still to be equalled. A newspaper cutting from 1938 reports on one of her wins: "After an interval to give her time to rest, she again went into slips together with the other finalist – a beautiful black dog called Haredam Arab (he has the same dam as Calliope). This was a course of exceptional length and although both hounds demonstrated their ability to a remarkable degree, Calliope gained a clear win. No matter how well Arab ran, he seemed unable to score against her. Calliope in all her coursing ways appeared to be the very double of her sire in the field. Both are white and although Calliope, being a bitch, is smaller, she is almost comically similar in every other feature, while her lovely action in galloping is Haredam Viking over again. Calliope is undoubtedly a great bitch and her win was immensely popular."

Early enthusiasts of the breed owning both show champions and winners on the coursing field were: Brigadier and Mrs Lance (Sarona); Commander Adams (Haredam); Mrs J. Mitchell (el Nablous); Mrs Crouch (Orchard); Captain E. Ames (of Ayot); Mrs I. Cleve; Miss S. Kerrison (of Iraq); Lt Col and Mrs Joyce

In 1978/79, for the first time in the history of the Saluki or Gazelle Hound Coursing Club, three sisters won the major coursing awards during the same season; the Cleve Trophy, the Kerrison Cup and the Sharif Trophy. Pictured left to right: Ch. Knightellington Melody, Knightellington Zoulaira (dam), Knightellington Portia and Persephone of Knightellington (lying down).

Cressing Badi-Saba (left): Bred and owned by Audrey Cullen. She was born in March 1980 out of Lusaki Commodore ex Lusaki Amber, her paternal grandparents were Burydown Diena of Lusaki and Ch. Almanza Kafiat. "Saba" started her career by winning her very first stake in 1981. She won the Moray Cup in 1981 (when her litter sister Cressing Beersheba was runner-up), repeated the triumph in 1982 and 1983, and was runner-up in 1984 and 1987. She won the Blanco Cup (Saluki v Deerhound) in 1981 and 1982 and divided it in 1983. She won the prestigious Victor Henderson Trophy in 1981/82, 1982/83 and 1983/84 – an unequalled record and a tribute to her consistency as in 1983/84, she ran at only six meetings. Saba has won every major trophy, some of them twice, except for the Lady Gardner puppy stake in which she was a semi-finalist. The Sharif, the only trophy to have eluded her, she finally won in 1985 after having a litter of puppies. Saba won the Veteran trophy in 1990.

*Ch. Yazid Burydown Yehudi:
One of the outstanding
coursing Salukis in the history
of the breed; bred by Mrs Hope
Waters and owned by Mrs
Chris Ormsby. He was sired by
Knightellington Esmail, another
legend on the coursing field,
out of Ch. Burydown Asphodel
Alanya bred by Mrs Burns. A
true dual-purpose hound,
winning Best in Show at the
Saluki or Gazelle Hound Club
Champion Show in 1973, and
Best Dog at the Saluki Club
Open Show in 1980 at the age
of eleven years. On the cours-
ing field he won the Sandpiper
Trophy in 1972, Cleve Trophy
in 1974 and was the runner up*

*in 1975, Moray Trophy in 1971 and 1972, the joint winner of the Kerrison in 1972 and the
winner in 1973, and won the Veteran Stakes in 1977.*   Diane Pearce

*Amena Viceroy of Anasazi:
"Gringo," owned by Andy
Chryssolor and bred by
Mary Long, from Can.
Eng. Ch. Burydown Furu-
dasht ex Ch. Amena
Morning Glory, won the
prestigious 32 dog three
day Moray Trophy in
Scotland three times in
succession at the ages of
five, six and seven, and on
the last occasion defeated
the Deerhound to win the
coveted Blanco Trophy.
Consistency has been the
watchword throughout his
long coursing career,
winning the Kerrison
Trophy twice and the*

*Sharif in 1984. He has also won the Beverley Cup, the Fairford Stake, the Askalam Trophy,
the Grantham Stake, the Victor Henderson Memorial Trophy in the 1986/87 season and
shared the trophy in 1988/89. Now a Veteran he has continued his successes, winning at the
ages of eight and nine, the Red Lodge Purse and the Dava Trophy.*

(Sammarra) and Mr and Mrs Henri van Laun (of Yemen). All Saluki enthusiasts must be indebted to these pioneers, who fully realised the antiquity and exquisite nature of the breed, and the necessity to keep the Saluki a dual-purpose hound. Coursing activities ceased in 1939, due to the war. In December 1956 Mr Lewis Renwick, the Secretary of the Saluki Club, organised the first official post-war meeting, which was held at Newnham, near Baldock. Twelve hounds, including two champions, were entered in the one stake, the Kerrison Cup, which was not completed. Since 1956 coursing has grown from strength to strength, and today demand for membership to the Coursing Section outstrips available places. The organisation of Saluki Coursing in the UK during the last decade owes a great deal to the hard work and enthusiasm of Brian Pether (Askalam), who retired from the Secretaryship during 1989.

All coursing is run by the Coursing Section of the Saluki or Gazelle Hound Club, based on rules administered by the National Coursing Club. Membership of the Coursing Section is restricted to a maximum of seventy, and they must be fully paid-up members of The Saluki or Gazelle Hound Club and the British Field Sports Society. Each member must also be the registered owner of any dog entered to course in a Stake. The waiting list for membership is around five years from the initial application, and the applicant is expected to have shown an interest in the sport by attending meetings and assisting in the field when requested. There are normally about twelve meetings held during the coursing season, which extends from September through to March. Each meet is divided into stakes of either eight, sixteen or thirty-two dogs. The most prestigious stakes competed for during the coursing season are: The Moray Cup, The Sharif Trophy, the Kerrison Stakes, The Cleve and the Lady Gardner Memorial Stakes (for Saluki puppies). Entry is by post with the draw being made about a week prior to the event. Each stake is usually specifically for either grade one and two dogs only, or for grade three and four dogs only. However, the top trophies are an exception, and they are open to all grades. Dogs are graded on their performance in the field as follows: grade one for dogs who have won a grade one-two stake; grade two for dogs who were runners-up in a grade one-two stake or who have won a grade three-four stake; grade three for dogs that have competed in a stake, and grade four for dogs that have never competed before.

There are two types of meetings held in the UK: the walk-up and the driven. At a walk-up meeting, all participants – "the field" – form a straight line, shoulder-to-shoulder with their hounds. They walk over the ground together, until a hare is flushed by the moving phalanx of dogs and humans. The slipper, wearing a red hunting jacket and positioned in front of the moving field, is alerted by a chorus of

"Hare!" He waits until the prey is some 75 metres away before loosing the Salukis for the chase. The running pair wear knitted woollen collars of either red or white. The "red collar" dog is always positioned on the left-hand side of the slipper; the "white collar" to the right. The slipper is licensed by the National Coursing Club, and he will only slip the brace on to a strong-running hare. The hares are always coursed over their own ground, belying the popular misconception that hares are brought in and released. This is, in fact, illegal. Usually single slips (one per dog) are used for walk-up meetings, and double slips (both dogs held side by side, with a single lead) are used for driven hunts.

At a driven meet the slipper positions himself behind cover, near the natural run of the hares. Beaters then drive the hares forward and past the slipper, who releases the dogs on to the running hare in the same manner as the walk-up. The field, largely reduced to spectating, are also positioned behind natural cover and away from the slipper. In all other respects, the procedure of the course is identical. Each stake is run as a simple knock-out competition. The winner of the first course will run against the winner of the second course, and so on, until the eventual winner is determined. To win the Sharif Trophy, which is thirty-two dog stake, the winner has to run five times in one day, a real test of fitness, endurance, ability, and stamina. The trophy for this stake was donated in 1964, in memory of Mrs Susan Hudson's Kumasi Sharif, a smooth Saluki bred by Mr and Mrs Henderson, who was unbeatable in his day. The judge, who always wears a red hunting jacket and is mounted on horseback, follows and points the running hounds under National Coursing Club guidelines. In Scotland, the judge is not mounted because the terrain is unsuitable for horses. Instead, he keeps ahead of the field in a position advantageous to judging, often on a hillside, following the course through field glasses. When the course is adjudged to be over, usually when the hare has gone to ground or has been killed, the judge will indicate the winner by raising either a red or a white handkerchief. The winner is the dog that scores the greater number of points.

Points are awarded by the judge for the dog's skill and persistence, and a pointing system has been designed to ensure that the hound which does the most work is the winner. The points of the course are:

Speed: 1, 2, or 3 points, according to the degree of superiority shown.

The go-bye: 2 points, or if gained on the outer circle 3 points. The go-bye is where a dog starts a clear length behind his opponent and yet passes him in a straight run and gets a clear length in front of him.

The turn: 1 point, this is where the hare is brought round at not less than a right angle from her previous line.

The line wading through thick heather at a combined Deerhound, Saluki meeting in the highlands of Scotland. This three day event was started in the fifties by coursing enthusiasts, notably Kenneth Cassels (pictured in the kilt), Lewis Renwick and Lt Cmmdr David and Hope Waters.

The wrench: half-a-point, this is where the hare is bent from its line at less than a right angle by the dog.

The kill: not more than 1 point, in proportion to the degree of merit displayed in that kill, which may be of no value.

The trip: 1 point, this is the unsuccessful effort to kill, where the hare is thrown off its legs, or where a dog flecks the hare but cannot hold it.

Perhaps the most popular event of the year is the combined three-day coursing meeting held in the Scottish Highlands with the Deerhound Coursing Club. In addition to those members with running dogs, it also attracts world-wide coursing enthusiasts as spectators. The scenery is spectacular, and many of the courses are absolutely thrilling. This event was started in the 1950s by a number of coursing enthusiasts, notably Kenneth Cassels, Lewis Renwick, and Hope and David Waters. Three stakes are run: The Moray Cup (32 dogs), The Moray Purse (16 dogs) for Salukis beaten in the first round of The Moray Cup, and The Dava Trophy (8 dogs) for Salukis beaten in the second round of The Moray Cup. The quarry is the Blue Mountain hare, which is slightly smaller than the brown hare coursed in England. The Deerhounds and Salukis are run alternately in pairs, until all the stakes have been completed. On the final day the winning Deerhound and Saluki, amid rival cheers from a partisan audience, compete against each other in the final run of the event for the Blanco Trophy. Over the years, both breeds have been evenly matched. The deep heather and grassy tussocks, which the hounds run over, slightly favour the Deerhound, and this counterbalances the Saluki's superior speed.

The importance of coursing in maintaining the Saluki as a pure-bred working dog is summed up by Michael Lyne, artist and Saluki owner, in his book *Coursing – The Pursuit Of Same With Gazehound:* "An awareness of the responsibility of maintaining the sporting characteristics of an animal, pure-bred for centuries, is indicated by the fact that comparatively little time elapsed between the importation of the first Saluki and the commencement of organised hare coursing with the breed in England. A dog so exotic in appearance could easily have appealed more to those who show dogs, or who wished for an ornamental companion. Luckily, there were at that time those who cherished their gazehounds as an inheritance and realised that the breeding for appearance's sake alone did not in all honour fulfil the role of custodian of this link with the past."

COURSING IN AMERICA

In America, hare coursing is called "open field coursing" to distinguish it from "lure coursing," which involves the pursuit of an artificial lure pulled electrically in a pre-determined and fixed pattern. The coursing season runs from late October until early March, under the rules of the National Open Field Coursing Association (NOFCA). This is a confederation of sighthound clubs which formulates the rules for the sport, approves judges, maintains the registry of eligible clubs, and awards point-based coursing championships (CCs) and other performance awards. Mixed sighthound and some Saluki-only coursing events are held during each season, culminating in the most prestigious event of the year, the "Grand Course." This is an invitation only event, usually held over two or possibly three days. The running hounds are the best representatives of each breed during that season. The invitations are highly-prized, and the winner is assured a place in American coursing history. Since its inception, only two Salukis have won the Grand Course: Can. Ch. Persia of Kahlil CC CM, a bitch owned by the Veynas in 1978, and Tallahamara Musdiy CC CM, owned by Herb Wells in 1990. The majority of coursing meetings are held in Central California, where the modern form of the sport originated in the early 1960s, due largely to the efforts of Dr Winifred Lucas (Srinagar Salukis) and Lyle Gillette (Rancho Gabriel Borzois and Salukis). In recent years, the North American Coursing Association (NACA) has been formed, and this offers formal coursing and points in

"Tally ho!" The start of a course at the 21st Annual NOFCA Grand Course, California, 1990.   *Darrell Black.*

the Rocky Mountain area. The premier event in their annual coursing calendar is the Whitetail Invitational.

There are several differences between American and British coursing. In America there are no driven meetings, only the walk-up – where the competitors and hounds form a line, known as the gallery, and walk forward, side-by-side, until the quarry is "put-up". Three hounds usually run in each individual course, wearing coloured jackets of pink, yellow or blue, as opposed to the two hounds in red or white collars

Tallahamara Musdiy CC CM: Musdiy, owned by Herb Wells, was the winner of the 1990 Grand Course, becoming the second Saluki to win this prestigious event, since it was first held in 1970.

Susan Schroder.

that are run in Britain. A beaten hound can still run in the finals if it scores sufficient points and distinguishes itself during its first course, whereas in Britain the dogs are eliminated on a knock-out basis. The judge is unmounted in America and handlers slip their own hounds on a command from the Huntsmaster, rather than having an official slipper to do the job. In most of the hunts, all the sighthound breeds compete against each other, while in Britain a Saluki competes against a Saluki. These mixed courses often provide some of the season's most exciting spectacles, as it is fascinating to observe the different running styles and strengths of the various breeds in competition against each other. Usually it is the Greyhound, Saluki and the Whippet that are the most competitive; the Saluki excels in a long-distance course, the Greyhound in the shorter run, where the sprint is usually the deciding factor, and the Whippet combines a little of both these attributes.

In California and throughout the Southwest, the quarry is the black-tailed jackrabbit, which is a lighter and faster animal than the English hare. In the Mountain States and Upper Midwest, the white-tailed jackrabbit is hunted. The whitetail is heavier than its lowland cousin, and it is similar in size, weight and appearance to the mountain hare of Scotland. Jackrabbits do not live in burrows, but in forms hollowed out at the base of sagebush or other low growth. They are the favourite prey of many predators, especially coyotes. This has made them exceedingly cunning, and they will sit completely silent and motionless, while the gallery and hounds walk over and around them. When they are being chased they can achieve running speeds of between 40 and 45mph. In the lowland fields of

California, the blacktail's preferred tactic is a swift dash to the long, straight roads that border the region's seemingly endless irrigation canals. If pressed by its pursuers, the jack will lay its highly mobile ears back flat onto its spine, lower its body parallel to within less than an inch of the ground and literally skim the surface of the earth. On the mile-high plains of the eastern slope of the Rockies, the whitetail's favourite diversion is the long, steady pull up the sage-covered inclines that rim the grassy valleys where it browses. Often the spectators' involvement ceases as the quarry leads the dogs up, over, and out of sight, off on unseen courses of sometimes incredible duration. Those that have attended or coursed in Scotland will be familiar with this scenario! A typical day's

The Gallery.

coursing in America begins with the competitors meeting at a prescribed point for the draw. Anyone may enter, so long as their dog is a pure-bred sighthound and is registered with NOFCA. All dogs compete in the first run – the preliminary. Successful hounds then run a second time in the final; the draw for this is carried out on the field. There is no division of breed (unless there is a specific disclaimer), or for dogs with or without open field titles – so different sighthounds breeds run in competition with each other, and novices can be drawn to compete with coursing champions. A huntsmaster and a field committee are also appointed before entering the hunting grounds. The committee consists of three people familiar with the current rules and regulations, and they are responsible for making decisions and settling any disputes that may arise. The huntsmaster establishes how the field is to

Am. Can. Ch. Srinagar Cirrus al Talat CC CM (Ch Srinagar Sunara Surya ex Ch. Srinagar Vara Hubini al Talat), 1969-1981. Bred by Jayne Harpling and Srinagar Kennels. Owned by Charles and Marion Alexander. Cirrus' pedigree was predominantly English, combining Srinagar's early imports and old Jen Araby lines. Natural speed, agility, and incred-

ible stamina enabled him to dominate Californian coursing for many seasons during the mid 1970's. His soundness, fluid movement, and relaxed nature made him a special favourite with sporting dog judges in the ring. CK Alexander.

Bayt Shahin Impulse CC CM: (Am. Can. Ch. Srinagar Cirrus al Talat, CC,CM ex Windswift Afri Bayt Shahin, CC, CM), 1975-1985. Bred and owned by Dr Daniel and Laura D. Belkin. Her matchless performances in the coursing field during the late 1970's are made more vivid in memory by her stunning whiteness. Fast, powerful, and fearless, she combined the best

talents of her sire and dam and her famous and equally formidable grandsire, Knightellington Esmail. Even now, to "run like Impulse" is the highest praise a new competitor can hope to hear.

C. K. Alexander.

Ch. El Char Azali Amir Ibn Isis CC CM: (Ch. Srinagar Cirrus al Talat,CC,CM ex El-Char's Al Qahirah Isis). Born in January, 1979, Azali burst on to the Californian coursing scene in the fall of 1980, winning five of his first eight hunts. During his first two coursing seasons he won thirteen out of twenty-six hunts, and was placed in most of the others, including both Grand Courses. He dominated Saluki open field coursing in California for six seasons, and won all four hunts in New Mexico. He is the second all-time high-scoring Saluki (behind only the Belkins' fabulous Impulse), and holds the leading position for most hunts won and most ASA coursing cups won.   Curt Ries.

be worked, keeps the gallery in order, directs the release of the dogs, and confers with the judge when necessary. If the entry is large enough, it is divided into two separate stakes using two different fields. Each field is run separately, with the winners of the two stakes running a third time to decide upon the overall winner.

On the field, the participants form into the gallery. The three dogs that are about to course are positioned in the best vantage point and slightly forward of the gallery. The field is then worked, under the instructions of the huntsmaster, the whole of the line moving forward at a slow pace to flush out the hare. When a hare is raised the gallery is expected to call "rabbit", and state the direction it is running, for example: "rabbit right", "rabbit left" or "rabbit behind". The huntsmaster looks for the hare and checks to see that the dogs about to be slipped are sighted before shouting "tally ho" – the release call. If he considers the hare should not be run, for any reason, he will not call the release. If he does give the call, it is the handler's responsibility to hold his dog until hearing the "T" of "Tally ho". If a dog is released prematurely, it can be penalised by losing one to ten points for what is called a "pre-slip". The released dogs then pursue the quarry, and their performance and skill in the chase is scored by the judge. The hounds are judged subjectively on speed, agility, and endurance, and they are given a numerical score. The judge either walks with the gallery or stands on a promontory watching each course through binoculars. On the completion of a course the dogs return to their owners, who join the gallery, and the next three to run take up their place "on the line". This routine continues throughout the day until all the dogs have run in the preliminary courses. The draw is then made for the final courses. The scores of each dog, recorded by the judge, form the basis for the final selection. He selects all of the dogs who won their preliminary course, and at his discretion, any other dog who has a score equal to or above the average score of the course winners. The judge's decision as to who runs in the finals is absolute. After the final runs are completed, the performance scores are tallied: preliminary and final scores are added together in order to achieve final placements of the hounds competing. In the case of ties there are no run-offs for the position – instead the points awarded for those places are added together and divided by the number of dogs tying for them; all the tied hounds are credited with the same score and placement.

American open field coursing continues to attract those who esteem the Saluki's heritage as a hunting breed. However, for a Saluki to succeed at coursing, a very high level of fitness is required. Competitive advantage depends on well-developed powers of endurance, as well as natural speed. When organised coursing first began in the Western USA, it was fairly common for Salukis to be coursed one weekend and shown successfully the next. In fact, many early coursing champions were also show champions. But as coursing has become increasingly competitive, the number of individual Salukis being shown and coursed has steadily declined. Currently, about ten per cent of coursing Salukis enter the show ring, and very few have succeeded in becoming "dual champions", attaining both their coursing and show titles.

NOFCA COURSING TITLES

American hounds qualify for the title of Coursing Champions by accumulating points from their various coursing wins. There is no equivalent award in Britain. Championship points are awarded to hounds placed in Regular Stakes, according to the following schedules:
1) First place: Four times the number of competing hounds in the stake, with a maximum of 40 points.
2) Second place: Three times the number of competing hounds in the stake, with a maximum of 30 points.
3) Third place: Two times the number of competing hounds in the stake, with a maximum of 20 points.

4) Fourth place: Points equal to the number of competing hounds in the stake, with a maximum of 10 points.

5) Fifth place: Points equal to half the number of competing hounds, with a maximum of 5 points.

Coursing Champion (CC)

The permanent title of Coursing Champion (CC) shall be awarded as a suffix to the registered name of any hound which has fulfilled the following championship qualifications:

1) Received 100 championship points.

2) Received at least 10 of the 100 points in a regular breed stake.

3) Received at least 10 of the 100 points in a regular mixed stake.

4) Received first place in a regular stake or two second places.

5) Received official credit for at least one unassisted kill or two assisted kills in any regular stake, breed or mixed.

Award of Coursing Merit (CM)

A permanent award of Coursing Merit (CM) shall be assigned as a suffix to the registered name of any hound which has fulfilled the following qualifications:

1) Received 100 championship points in regular breed stakes, or by earning high-score breed awards in NOFCA sponsored hunts.

2) Received first place in a regular breed stake or two second places.

3) Received official credit for at least one unassisted take or two assisted takes in a regular hunt.

4) Kill credits can be taken from either breed or mixed stakes.

LURE COURSING

Lure coursing is very popular in the United States, Canada, Europe and several other countries around the World, where live hare coursing is banned. There are very few lure coursing events held in Britain for Salukis, and those organised are usually fun events. Recently, however, a sighthound lure coursing club has been set up under the auspices of The British Sighthound Field Association. This has attracted a strong following, and dogs are run in competition with each other, under strict rules.

Lure field trials consist of two, or three, hounds chasing an artificial lure (often sheets of coloured plastic) attached to a nylon wire and pulled electronically in a prescribed pattern, dictated by the placement of pulleys set into the ground. The course incorporates swoops, dips and turns, and the hounds always start and finish at

Greendale Saudamani Jamilll FCH: (Shamsir Saudamani Xenophon ex Bayt Shahin et Voila). In March 1989, thirteen months after his first birthday, Jami ran in his first field trial and won Best of Breed. He finished his Field Championship in six trials. By May 1990 he had won all but a few of his Lure Courser of Merit points with a total of eight Best in Fields. Jami, bred by Julia Holder and Ingrid Brown and owned by Ruth and Jack Southam, is the careful breeding and blending of English and American show and coursing Salukis. Jami is a beautiful, small, muscular and extremely fit athlete, with a loving and high spirited temperament.

the same point. The distance of the course is designed to test the ability and the endurance of the Saluki. The ideal lure course for a Saluki would be between 1000 to 1500 yards, although 2000 yards should not be ruled out. The course should include a fast run-up of about 500 yards, with sufficient turns in the remaining distance to test the Saluki's ability. It is exciting to watch, but very different from live hare coursing, which demands different skills from the Saluki. Live coursing is held in almost all weather conditions, over diverse terrain or running grounds, and the hounds are tested by the agility, cunning, strength and speed of the quarry. Lure coursing normally takes place in a large enclosed field, in good weather, and the synthetic quarry always moves in the same fixed pattern, usually reversed for the second run. The hounds are expected to follow the lure's every move around the course; those cutting corners or anticipating turns are penalised by the judge. This can sometimes be a problem for the intelligent Saluki if the second run is not reversed, as they will remember each turn and twist and adjust their running pattern to anticipate the route of the lure. The Salukis thoroughly enjoy themselves, but some have a tendency to run just fast enough to keep ahead of the opposition, or to keep reasonably close to the lure. A good lure operator, by careful control and acceleration of the speed of the lure, can really stretch and test the ability of the Saluki to the full.

In hot pursuit after the lure, Lexington, Kentucky.

Saudamani Sabeel LCM II: (Shamsir Saudamani Xenophon ex Ch Bayt Shahin Saudamani Jehana FCH). Beel, owned and bred by Ruth and Jack Southam, has run for five of his six years with great consistency; always in the ribbons. Winning thirty first placements, nineteen Best of Breeds and five Best in Fields during his lure coursing career. After his retirement he had the honour to win the AKC Coursing Dog Class (lure and open field), which was being offered for the first time ever to Salukis at the National Specialty, Lexington, Kentucky, in June 1990. Beel is from a litter of eight and was born dead. After futile attempts to bring breath to his little body, he was carefully wrapped in newspaper and placed in a covered plastic container. Several hours later the Southams heard squeals and rustlings; he was alive and kicking...

Ch. Montebell Sherom's Irish Boy LCM: (Am. Can. Ch. Montebello's Tinniin Kaihorn ex Ch. Montebello Sedeki Shahriin). "Irish" is owned by Tom and Shereen Shuman and bred and co-owned by Katharine L. Sauerman. In 1987 and 1988 he was the number one lure coursing Saluki and was fourth in 1989, the same year he obtained his show title. Irish is the first Saluki to be a number one lure courser and Specialty Breed winner, he has earnt three Lure Courser of Merit titles and is well on his way to his fourth LCM title.

In America the Sighthound Field Association (ASFA) was founded in 1972, setting up rules and regulations to govern the sport. Its objective was to preserve and develop the natural beauty, grace, speed and coursing skills of pure-bred sighthounds. Most of the Salukis who participate in American lure coursing events also compete in the show ring, with approximately one third of them becoming show champions. Under ASFA rules, hounds are judged and scored (maximum total of 100 points) for the following abilities:

Enthusiasm (15 points): The desire and determination to catch the lure in pursuit.

Speed (25 points): The rate at which a hound can traverse turns, as well as changes in terrain. Speed also includes acceleration, which is the rate at which a dog can go from a complete stop to maximum speed.

Follow (15 points): The ability of a hound to pursue the lure, keeping it in sight at all times. Dogs are frequently penalised for not watching the lure or for anticipating where the lure is going.

Agility (25 points): The ability to change direction or speed while still keeping the lure in sight.

Endurance (20 points): The ability to complete a course without an appreciable loss of speed or agility.

Judges award points to each dog up to the maximum number allowed in each section. Penalty points of 1 to 10 can also be deducted for slipping too soon, or for a delay in the dog's entering slips. A Field Champion (FCH) title is awarded to a Saluki or sighthound that wins two first placements, or one first placement and two second placements in competition, as well as attaining 100 championship points. Champion points are awarded in proportion to the number of dogs competing, with a maximum of 40 points awarded for first place. Points are calculated as follows:

First place – four times the number of hounds competing in the stake (maximum of 40 points).

Second place – three times the number of hounds competing in the stake (maximum of 30 points).

Third place – two times the number of hounds competing in the stake (maximum 20 points).

Fourth place – points equal to the number of hounds competing in the stake (maximum 10 points).

A Lure Courser of Merit (LCM) title is awarded to a Saluki or sighthound that wins four first placements in competition and 300 points (in addition to those obtained earning their FCH title). Multiple Lure Courser of Merit titles are awarded each time a hound repeats this feat. For example: the second time it is achieved the title LCM II is awarded, the third time LCM III, and so on. From 1976 until the end of 1989, only twenty Salukis in America have earned the LCM II title, which is an indication of how difficult it is to achieve.

Chapter Ten

BREEDING

Breeding from your Saluki is not a decision that should be taken lightly, and that applies equally to owners of male and female Salukis. All Saluki owners play an important role in preserving the quality of future generations. It is not just a case of letting your dog be used on any bitch that comes along, pocketing the stud fee, and considering that your responsibility is at an end. You may feel flattered because someone wants to use your dog as a potential sire, but think about the implications, and be realistic. Your dog may have been selected simply because you live conveniently close to the owner of the bitch. If you care enough about the breed and the intrinsic qualities of your own dog, you should be circumspect about the bitch that is being presented for mating. Do the pedigrees match, or if it is an outcross, do the dog and bitch complement each other? After all, your dog's name is going to be on that pedigree and everyone with an interest in the breed will be evaluating your dog's offspring. If you have reservations about the proposed mating, on grounds of lines, type, soundness, temperament or whatever, be prepared to stand up for your beliefs and principles.

The main responsibilities of breeding, however, do fall on the owner of the bitch. Breeding a litter of puppies can be both rewarding and fun, but it is a major

A male and female Saluki: both are good, sound specimens of the breed.

undertaking. It is irresponsible to contemplate producing a litter without any firm buyers in mind. Commonsense should tell you that it is both cruel and undesirable to bring unwanted puppies into a limited market-place. The prospect of placing Salukis in good, caring and understanding homes is very limited, and you certainly will not make any financial profit out of the enterprise if you raise the litter correctly. Equally, it is morally wrong to sell the puppies, either on the cheap or to unsuitable homes. Your obligation to the litter does not end with the sale. You must be prepared to answer and solve any problems that the purchaser may have, and in some cases, you may have to take back puppies housed in unsuitable homes or no longer wanted because of breakdown in marriage or illness and bereavement. Saluki breed clubs throughout the world have a very good rescue system for unwanted Salukis, providing a magnificent service, but they should not have to take on your responsibilities as a breeder. Breeding from poor stock is imprudent and does not contribute to the well-being of the breed. Breeding, if you are to do it correctly, is expensive and involves a lot of hard work. If you cannot afford to do it properly, or you are not prepared to devote the necessary time and attention to detail – don't try. It is much easier to buy in another puppy.

If you are still intent on breeding a litter, it should be emphasised that your bitch must be healthy, sound, and have a good temperament. Never breed from a bitch with a major health or temperament problem – this is totally irresponsible. The general aim of successful breeding is to reproduce offspring that comply to the Breed Standard – the ideal dog displaying moderation in all points rather than extremes. The bitch should therefore be a good specimen of the breed, meeting most, if not all, of the criteria of the Breed Standard. Before mating, the bitch should be checked over by the vet to establish that she is in good health, and if you have been in the habit of suppressing the seasons, make sure that she has one normal "heat" before breeding from her. It is generally considered to be a good idea to worm and revaccinate the prospective brood bitch against distemper, hardpad, hepatitis, leptospirosis and canine parvovirus before the mating. This will increase the immunity that the mother will pass on to the litter during the critical and vulnerable early weeks.

SELECTING A STUD DOG

Selecting a suitable stud dog needs careful research into the various bloodlines that are available. It is this detailed knowledge of pedigrees, plus the experience of seeing dogs in the ring and recalling their faults and qualities, that usually gives the experienced breeder a higher degree of success. You should resist the temptation of

Ch. Kaus Kezia (Int. Ch. Sedeki Barre ex Ch. Mazuri Lail) left, with two of her children, Ch. Pennyworth Riaz and Ch. Pennyworth Katiya.

Ch. Timotheus of Chandav (Ch. Al Caliphs Alyfeh ex Ch. Rachel of Chandav) Dog World's Top Saluki Stud Dog 1985, 1986, 1987.

going to the top winning dog of the day; it may have the same faults as your bitch or be bred from completely different bloodlines. Your choice of dog should compliment any deficiencies that your bitch may have: e.g. don't put a bad front to a bad front – this, in all probability, will only duplicate the fault. The owner of the stud dog will require a fee for the service; which will have to be negotiated. Most fees include two matings, and if a bitch fails to conceive, a repeat mating next time she is in season. Terms and conditions vary and must be agreed beforehand, and if necessary, a written contract should be signed. In some instances, the owner of the stud dog will decide to have a puppy in place of a fee.

When you are planning a litter there are three different types of breeding programmes to be considered: in-breeding, line-breeding and outcrossing. In-breeding should only be contemplated by breeders with many years experience, as it involves the pairing together of close relations: sire to daughter, dam to son, or brother to sister. The aim is to duplicate and fix the best points within the line. Unfortunately, bad genes are just as likely to be duplicated, and a recessive fault can appear within the breeding. Line-breeding is another selective form of breeding. It is more of a happy medium and establishes a similarity of type. The idea is to maintain a close link throughout the pedigrees, breeding only dogs of the highest standard together: i.e. cousins, uncles, aunts, nieces and nephews, rather than the very close links of in-breeding. If your bitch has been carefully bred along these line principles, it is probably a good idea to continue on this course, as long as you don't select a sire that is too closely related. Line-breeding is usually the most favoured by established breeders. Out-crossing is where unrelated dogs are used, predominantly to improve or to introduce a feature that is lacking within a particular line. Sometimes it is used if the breeding has got too close, and fresh bloodlines need to be introduced.

There is a lot of skill involved in choosing a suitable dog and balancing the future litter's pedigree so that faults are reduced and good points are emphasised. Successful breeders tend to combine and use the best features of both line-breeding and out-crossing in order to improve their stock. First-time breeders, who need advice on this complex matter, should go back to the breeder of their bitch – his or her experience could be invaluable in helping you make the right decisions.

WHEN TO BREED FROM YOUR BITCH

Although a bitch is capable of conception from her first season, veterinary opinion considers it most unwise and imprudent to breed with her so early. Because of the bitch's immaturity, she would be unlikely to raise the litter successfully without endangering her own health and growth potential, and in all probability, some of the litter might die. Mating should not be considered until the bitch is two to two and a half years of age. Most Saluki breeders favour waiting until the bitch is between four and five years of age, because Salukis are reckoned to be a slow-maturing breed. If you are contemplating breeding from a maiden bitch who is over the age of seven, it is best to seek veterinary advice before making the decision. It is an obvious risk to the bitch's health, and the well-being of the resulting puppies may also be affected.

The bitch comes into season at regular intervals, the frequency varying from between six to twelve months. It is important to note the date of the first blood-stained discharge from the season, as the mating day is calculated from this time. However, this can only serve as a guide, unless you have witnessed and kept close observations of previous seasons. Our bitches are usually at their most fertile between the seventeenth and nineteenth day of their season. Others may be ready between the tenth and thirteenth day. Biologically, the optimum day for mating and high fertility is just before the bitch ovulates. This is usually indicated by the vagina softening and becoming enlarged. The bitch will also stand and turn her tail aside, to invite copulation. If you are unsure about evaluating the appropriate day, your vet can take a series of vaginal smears or do a blood test to assess the stage of the cycle and advise on the correct day for mating. If you have a dog of your own on the premises, he will certainly inform you when the time is right.

THE MATING

It is normal practice to take the bitch to the dog for the mating. If both the owners are inexperienced, it is a good idea to invite someone to come along who is knowledgeable in the procedure. Mating is a natural process; it is normally preceded by a period of flirtatious play, to precipitate physical stimulus. When the bitch is ready she will stand and 'tail' for the dog. The dog will then mount the bitch, gripping her with his forelegs, and penetrate her with his penis. If the bitch is a maiden this can be painful; she will involuntarily cry out and try to move away from the dog. A tight grip on her collar by the owner will stop this from happening. After ejaculation, part of the dog's penis swells up to keep it in place. The dog will now climb off the bitch, turn around and stand back-to-back with her, but still joined together. The dog may need some gentle assistance to accomplish this move, and it may be necessary to reassure and hold the couple; if the bitch panics and pulls away it can harm the dog.

The tie normally lasts for about twenty minutes or until the dog's penis relaxes and they separate from each other naturally. The bitch should then be taken away and allowed to rest. It is possible to have a fertile mating without the tie, so long as the dog has remained within the bitch long enough for the sperm to be deposited. It is common practice to have a second mating within a period of two days. The stud fee is normally paid immediately after the mating, and a receipt, a copy of the dog's pedigree and its stud book number should be obtained. The owner of the stud dog will also have to sign the official Kennel Club form to confirm the mating. This form is eventually sent to the Kennel Club when the resulting litter is registered.

PREPARING FOR WHELPING

The first essential item is a whelping box, and this can be constructed quite easily, using timber obtained from the local DIY store. The basic requirements are that it should be large enough to allow the bitch to stretch out, turn around, stand up and get out of – while at the same time allowing the puppies to move around unrestricted as they grow older. The sides should be high enough to restrain the pups from climbing over the top. The whole floor area of the box should be covered with layers of newspaper and the use of a VetBed in the top half of the accommodation will make it more comfortable for the mother. The box should be located in a quiet area of the house where mother and pups will not be disturbed unnecessarily. The bitch should be introduced to the whelping box a few days before the puppies are due, if only for short periods, so she has a chance to get used to her new accommodation.

It will probably be necessary to provide some form of heating to keep the puppies warm, especially during the night. Some breeders use an infra-red light suspended over the whelping box. The temperature is controlled by either raising or lowering the light. The disadvantage of this method of heating is that it tends to be dry, and the bitch can sometimes become too hot and has to leave the box. An alternative is to use a flat electrically-heated pad and place it under the blanket, ensuring that the cable is fed through a hole in the floor of the box and is out of reach of any inquisitive puppy, who might be tempted to nibble at the flex.

PREGNANCY

It is unlikely that you will notice any external differences in your bitch for at least four weeks, although we have been able to detect minor behavioural changes in our own bitches during this period. The first sign is usually the enlargement of the abdomen; this can be detected by a slight filling out of the flanks. Pregnancy lasts, on average, sixty-three days, but litters can be born seven days either side of this time-scale. The pregnant bitch does not require any additional food until about five weeks into her pregnancy. Her normal diet will suffice. As the pregnancy advances and the unborn puppies grow, the bitch will require additional food. Protein levels will need to be raised, increasing the level by about one-third to one half in quantity. She will require a good wholemeal cereal, egg, cheese, and meat (both raw and cooked), as well as cod-liver oil (best fed in capsule form), and a form of calcium – such as Stress. As the pregnancy advances the stomach will be displaced by the swelling uterus, and the bitch will feel uncomfortable if she tries to eat a large meal. Meals should be offered two or three times a day, rather than all at once, and the more concentrated it is, the better. Try to provide the maximum of nourishment with the minimum of bulk. The bitch will still require exercise, but let her decide how much she wants to take. Our pregnant bitches are allowed their normal freedom to run in the garden. Salukis are usually natural mothers and are quite adept at looking after themselves, so long as you appreciate and understand their requirements. Towards the end of gestation, regular short walks are okay, but never let the bitch become over-tired.

As parturition draws near, the breasts swell and the nipples will enlarge and darken. The bitch will also take to digging. This is quite natural, for in the wild she would prepare a nest for her expected litter, It is also advisable to inform your vet of the expected whelping date. Although most births are quite normal, sometimes complications can set in and a caesarian section may be necessary. Other tell-tale signs that the whelping is drawing near are:

* The bitch's temperature will be slightly lower than normal (38C) during the last week of pregnancy. In the last twenty-four hours it will drop further to about 36C.
* Most bitches will refuse food in the last twenty-four hours.
* There is usually a discharge of a green mucus from the vagina about two hours prior to whelping.
* The bitch will become restless and will probably commence deep, nervous panting.

All you can do is to be sympathetic and consoling, very much like an expectant father – the miracle of birth is imminent. There are a number of items that you should have ready:

* Your vet's telephone number, day and night.
* Plenty of old newspapers, but only the absorbent type (Sunday supplements are no good).
* Two good-quality fibre blankets: SnugRug or VetBed are both safe and easy to wash.
* Paper towels.
* A clean face flannel.
* A skin disinfectant for your hands.
* Scales.
* Scissors.
* A notebook and pen to record birth-weights etc.

WHELPING

Whelping is, or should be, a natural and normal process. The puppies are attached throughout gestation to the uterine horn by the placenta – the umbilical cord connecting puppy and placenta. The placenta, cord and puppy (whelp) are enclosed in a membrane sac. This sac, contains a fluid which acts as a cushion to protect the whelp from damage during the birth process. The bitch will probably be able to cope with the whole process of whelping, with a minimum of assistance. The first stage of labour can last for twelve hours or even longer. The bitch will be restless, frequently rearrange her bed and pant. During this period, the contractions are not powerful or regular, and should not distress the bitch unduly.

Stage two commences with the first major contraction; this is much stronger than those previously witnessed. It is a good idea to make a note of the time this occurs. If the first puppy has not appeared after an hour, you should contact your veterinary surgeon for advice. The first indication of the new arrival is the appearance of a dark-coloured sac of fluid (the water bag) at the vulva. The next contraction should expel the puppy still in its foetal membranes. Don't panic if the puppy arrives feet-first – about forty per cent of births are breech. If there is a little difficulty with the birth, some gentle assistance can be given. Hold the puppy's head or hindlegs with a clean, dry, face flannel and pull down gently and away from the spine. Try to pull in unison with the bitch's contractions and don't use undue force – this could cause serious damage.

The bitch should instinctively tear open the sac, bite the cord and lick the puppy clean and dry. If she fails to do this, you will have to do it for her. Clear the membrane away from its nose, cut the umbilical cord with your fingers or with clean scissors. Rub the wet whelp vigorously to dry it, and place it on a nipple. Take care when cutting the cord, because if this is done incorrectly it could result in a hernia. The correct way is to pinch the cord in the thumb and forefinger of the right hand, about one and a half inches away from the puppy's body, then do the same with the left hand – the thumbs should touch. Pull with the right hand towards the whelp, keeping the left hand still: never pull away from the puppy's body. The puppy's placenta, or afterbirth may come out with the whelp, or follow up to fifteen minutes later. The bitch will usually eat the placenta and clean up the fluids emitted during the birth. Eating the placentas will not do the bitch any harm, but if it is a large litter, it is better if she does not eat them all. A note should be made of the number of placentas passed; there should be one for each puppy born. A placenta retained within the bitch after labour has finished can be very dangerous – contact the vet if this happens. It is a good idea to record each puppy's birth weight, and then continue to weigh the pups daily. This will help you to spot any puppy that is not gaining in weight, and enable you to take the necessary action.

The second puppy can follow any time up to two hours after the first. The procedure is the same as for the first and any subsequent puppies, until whelping is complete. Ensure that each puppy finds a teat and starts suckling straight away, as the first few meals provide valuable protective colostral antibodies to combat disease during the early weeks. The mother is likely to get very thirsty, so water, with some glucose and milk added, should always be available. Contact your vet if there is a two hour delay between births, or telephone him immediately if there are any apparent complications with any of the deliveries.

After it is all over, the mother should settle down with her litter around her. By now she will be hungry, and something light, like an egg custard, is an ideal first meal. Now you can sit back, have a drink to celebrate, and embark on one of the biggest time-wasters ever – puppy-watching!

Chapter Eleven

RAISING A SALUKI LITTER

THE FIRST TWO WEEKS

There should be very little need for human involvement following the safe delivery of the litter, and for the next three weeks the mother will be doing all the hard work. To begin with, she will sleep a lot, recovering from the physical exertion of the birth. For some weeks after the delivery, she will have a discharge from her vulva. At first the emission is a dark-green mucoid material, which will lighten to an odourless brown or reddish substance before becoming a clear mucus. This is quite normal. The danger signs are if the discharge becomes dark, mucky and foul-smelling, or persists beyond fourteen to twenty days. The bitch will probably show little interest in her puppies or her food, and she may be feverish and thirsty. This could indicate that a placenta or dead puppy has been retained inside her, causing metritis, which is an infection of the uterus. If you suspect a problem, contact your vet. He will give the bitch a thorough examination and, if necessary, he will prescribe a course of

Two day old Saluki puppy, the dew claws have still to be removed.

The eyes are just beginning to open at ten days.

antibiotics. Do not waste any time if you suspect the bitch is suffering from metritis: it can be fatal if it is not treated.

Within twenty-four hours of giving birth, the bitch should once again be interested in eating and drinking. Her protein requirements will be greater than a normal diet would allow, so it is a good idea to continue with the menu established during gestation. The best guide is the overall appearance of your bitch. If she is looking thin and lethargic her diet may need to be adjusted. During the first couple of weeks the litter will need food, peace and quiet, a warm environment that is free from draughts – and little else. Obviously, you should keep an eye on the pups, and ensure that each puppy is getting enough milk. If necessary, transfer a weaker-looking puppy on to a more productive nipple; some teats may have a better supply of milk. The well-being of the litter is very dependent on the quantity and quality of the dam's milk; so if she is experiencing any difficulties in producing enough milk, you may have to feed the puppies yourself (see Hand-Rearing). The mother will keep the puppies clean and will also clear up their faeces after them. You should, however, change the newspapers and VetBed in the whelping box regularly. Apart from food, warmth is the next most important factor in the early life of the young puppies. Supplementary heat should be provided during the first weeks as the puppies don't develop an efficient control over their own heat-regulation system until about four weeks of age. Keep the room temperature at around 30C-32C, dropping the room temperature by 3C every two weeks until the ambient temperature is achieved.

Healthy puppies should look plump and contented, with normal skin tension. They should be gaining weight slowly but progressively each day. It is a good idea to monitor each individual's weight on a daily basis. A contented litter will emit a chorus of gentle murmuring, only squealing loudly if they get knocked off a teat or the mother accidently treads on them. Although research indicates that puppies which are handled daily are more emotionally stable and resistant to stress, it is advisable to restrict access to family and close friends during these early weeks. It is essential that you also exercise stringent hygienic practices to reduce the possibility of introducing disease into the puppies' environment. For example, if you have been to a dog show or been in contact with strange dogs always wash your hands thoroughly before handling the puppies. It is also a good idea to change your external clothing and remove outdoor shoes before entering the puppy room.

The dew-claws should be removed during the first two or three days. Your vet will come and do this for you, and he can check the mother at the same time. The puppies' nails grow surprisingly quickly, and if they are not trimmed, the pups may scratch the bitch with the kneading movements they make while feeding. It is an easy job to keep them trimmed with a pair of nail scissors. The puppies can neither

Mother with babies, circa 16 days of age.

see nor hear during the first ten to fourteen days, and it takes another seven before they can focus properly. Hearing starts from between thirteen and seventeen days.

THREE TO EIGHT WEEKS

After about three weeks, life starts to get more hectic. The puppies can now see and hear, and will be starting to stagger around the whelping box – from now on there will never be a dull moment in the puppy room. If everything is going well, the puppies will feed quite happily from the dam until about five weeks of age, but it is a good idea to encourage the litter to lap milk from a saucer at about three weeks. We normally use goat's milk, which contains more protein and fat than cow's milk. At first, the puppies will step or stumble into the saucer and make a terrible mess, but soon they will be lapping quite successfully. When this stage is reached, the quantity of the milk can be increased (as a consequence reducing the strain on the bitch's milk bank), and this prepares the way for the next stage in the weaning process.

Milk teeth start to appear when the puppies are about three weeks of age, and you can introduce solids to their diet from about four weeks. A mixture of Farex, milk and honey makes a good starter-meal. Encourage the pups to eat by dipping your finger into the mixture and then placing your finger into their mouths. As the puppies learn to lap properly and eat sufficient quantities from their dish, you can introduce meat to the diet. The majority of Saluki breeders recommend scraped best stewing steak. To scrape the meat, lay a piece of steak flat out and draw a sharp knife across the surface, collecting a fine paste-like meat ball. These balls can then be fed individually to each puppy. Specially formulated puppy meat can be served as an alternative, but make sure you follow the manufacturer's instructions very carefully. Egg custard is another great favourite, and very few Salukis have been known to refuse it. However, never feed uncooked white of an egg to the puppies – it is almost indigestible. From about three and a half weeks of age, the puppies should have a supply of fresh water available at all times.

Normally, the puppies should be completely weaned by about five weeks. Meals should be fed four times a day, gradually increasing the quantity. Ensure that each puppy gets its fair share of food, especially if it is feeding from a communal bowl. Starchy foods should be avoided until the puppies are about six weeks old. It is better to concentrate on the highly nutritious foodstuffs already mentioned.

PLAY-TIME

At about five weeks of age, a healthy litter of puppies will be into everything, playing in short bursts of hectic activity. Playtime is important to their development: it gives them the opportunity to explore their surroundings and their relationships with humans and other canine members of the family. Most mothers will be happy to join in and contribute to their fun and their learning processes. If the litter has been reared indoors, without an outdoor run, it is essential that they get some fresh air. The garden will be a source of magical interest to the puppies, but you will need to keep an attentive eye on their activities. It doesn't matter how careful you are, you can guarantee that at least one of the pups will get into mischief, and we have seen Saluki puppies swimming in shallow fish ponds, halfway up trees, semi-submerged down small holes in the ground, with only a tail showing above the surface! As the puppies play, they are also establishing relationships between themselves, and the numerous tussles and tug-of-war contests that you witness will eventually decide a pack leader. A puppy's concentration span is very small, and each activity is short-lived, occupying a brief moment, before it finds something new to investigate – and this is all carried out at a speed reminiscent of old-time movies. It is almost impossible to photograph a litter at play. The best results you can get are brief cameos – then it's all over, the puppies fall into an exhausted sleep, and peace descends.

Puppies are very inquisitive.

Fortunately rest times are quite frequent.

Mum or Dad will often join in the fun.

WORMING

Nearly all puppies have roundworm, passed on through their mother, and this occurs even though you have wormed the dam during pregnancy. It is normal to start worming the puppies at about three weeks of age, repeating the dose every two to three weeks – but follow your own vet's advice on this.

VACCINATIONS

All puppies need protection from a range of diseases that could cause serious damage or could prove fatal. An inoculation course against distemper, hepatitis, leptospirosis and parvovirus is usually started at around eight weeks of age. Again, it is best to seek professional advice, as every veterinary practice has its own recommended programmes.

HAND-REARING

Some puppies may need to be hand-reared if the dam is not producing enough milk. This can happen if she has a specific problem or if she has a very large litter. For the most part, this is a matter of supplementing feeds. Sometimes, however, a breeder is faced with the dreaded scenario of the mother dying during delivery. This happened to us with the very first litter we bred, and, not surprisingly, we were totally unprepared to deal with the situation. But when you are faced with a crisis, it is amazing how quickly you learn to adapt.

It all started when our bitch, Abi (Jazirat Bey Sadi), was taken in for a caesarian operation, as her first puppy was jammed in the neck of the womb. During the course of the operation her heart failed, and although four veterinary surgeons worked for an hour, reviving her twice, she finally died. This life-or-death struggle had gone on without our knowledge. We arrived at the surgery, fully expecting to collect a proud mother and her litter. We were absolutely devastated at our loss. However, the entire litter had survived – three dogs and two bitches – but they were obviously cold, lying in a cardboard box. We later discovered that they had been put to one side, with no additional heating, and had virtually been forgotten during the fight for Abi's life. They had had one suckle from the mother, hopefully receiving at least some of the valuable colostrum, which might have given them some antibody immunity to combat disease.

Our grief at losing Abi was so intense that the pressing needs of the puppies were in danger of being overlooked. We were totally ill-equipped to deal with the situation both emotionally and practically. Fortunately, a fellow dog-breeder (a nurse) lived close to the surgery, and we called on her, on the journey home. She provided us with a few essentials, and more importantly, she wrapped each puppy in silver-foil to prevent further heat-loss. By this stage, the puppies were lying on a blanket, which was wrapped around a hot-water bottle When we got home, we fed the puppies a mixture of brandy, glucose and water, together with a mixture of milk, fed from an ink-dropper. After that first traumatic feeding session, the litter soon fell asleep and we embarked upon our labour of love and dedication. It was now our top priority to keep all of the puppies alive, whatever the cost, so we could retain something of our beloved Abi. Hasty 'phone calls to leading Saluki breeders, and frantic reading of a limited supply of books, established a list of priorities. We then set off on a shopping trip to purchase the equipment that had been established as essential, if we were to succeed. Unwittingly, we were now on the road to raising probably the first orphan hand-reared Saluki litter in the UK. We were offered a foster mother that was in milk, but by this stage we were committed to rearing the litter ourselves.

Hand rearing is by no means an easy task. It requires immense patience, dedication, time, planning – and loss of sleep. We outlined four critical areas in our rearing programme:

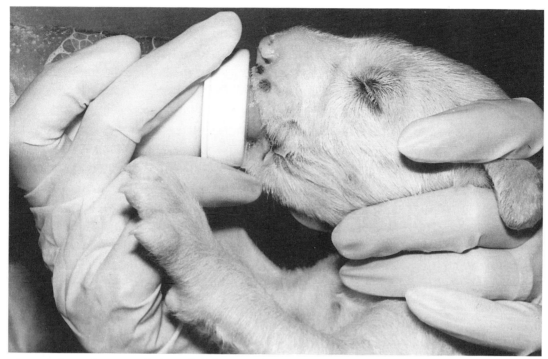

An orphaned puppy being fed from a bottle. It is interesting to note the kneading action of the paw against the hand.

1) The puppies must be kept at the right temperature and humidity at all times.
2) They must be carefully fed at regular intervals throughout the day and night.
3) They must pass water and motions regularly, and be kept spotlessly clean.
4) They must be kept in near-quarantine conditions to minimise the risk of infection.

Certain items of equipment were equally essential: baby's feeding bottles, spare feeding teats, an eye dropper, a plastic syringe, a plastic funnel, a fine wire-mesh tea strainer, feeding-bottle steriliser, petroleum jelly, milk of magnesia, a box of disposable surgical gloves, cotton wool, a room thermometer, a veterinary thermometer, Whelpi, disinfectant, two or more VetBeds, and a large supply of newspapers.

Room temperature

It is vital to keep the puppies warm, and we used an infra-red lamp and maintained an environmental temperature of between 29C and 32C. To ensure humidity, which is very important, we placed a bowl of cold water in the puppy room.

Feeding

We fed our litter on Whelpi, which is a scientifically formulated milk powder, which is as similar as possible to the real thing. We mixed the milk in the baby's feed bottles, carefully following the instructions provided. The only problem we encountered was that sometimes the powder didn't dissolve properly, which caused the teat to clog, and resulted in a very angry puppy at feeding time. This problem was overcome by mixing the milk separately and straining it through a fine tea-strainer, pulping down the excess powder and re-straining. The Whelpi formula contains all the necessary vitamins, so no other supplements were required. Precise quantities were fed to each puppy, and the milk was served at a temperature of 38C. Our timetable was strictly adhered to, always feeding at the correct intervals. For the first seven days we fed every two hours throughout twenty-four hours, and from eight to fourteen days we fed every three hours. At eighteen days we started the weaning procedure, which is several days earlier than if the litter had been suckling from the dam.

When we were hand-feeding, we used a standard baby's bottle fitted with a small teat. We did not get on very well with the bottles that were specially designed for animals. All the litter, with one exception, suckled well from the onset. The bad performer in the family was fed for the first three days with an eye dropper. The puppies were fed one at a time; and for the first three days they each consumed approximately half an ounce of milk at every feed. From three to five days, they were taking approximately one ounce, and from seven to ten days this was increased to about two and a half ounces. From fourteen days onwards the amount was around three ounces. These quantities were the only deviation from the manufacturer's recommendations.

When feeding with a bottle, the puppy should be held in the left hand, which is placed under its stomach. The right hand should support the puppy's head and the bottle. The puppy should be inclined slightly upwards so it can knead with its paws. We had to be careful not to overfeed or to feed too quickly, as this could make the pup feel uncomfortable and could induce vomiting.

After the puppy had finished eating, we used a dampened piece of cotton wool to remove any milk that had adhered to their faces during feeding. We also winded them to prevent colic and bellyache. This was carried out by gently rubbing their backs and stomach simultaneously to stimulate burping. We were also assisted by our Toy Poodle, who came in at feeding times and adopted the pups, giving each a thorough licking and buffeting!

Cleanliness of the litter

For the first twenty-one days or so, we made sure that every puppy urinated and defecated after feeding. Under normal circumstances, the mother stimulates the motions by licking. We duplicated this action by gently massaging the puppy's perineal and anal regions with a small piece of cotton wool which had been moistened in warm water. Afterwards,we applied a small amount of petroleum jelly to the genitals to prevent the skin becoming excoriated by urine. If there was any sign of constipation, we administered orally 0.5ml of milk of magnesia, using a syringe (minus the needle, of course), which was placed into the mouth and gently squeezed until all of the liquid had passed down the throat. The whelping box was kept clean and fresh, with the newspapers being changed after every meal and the VetBed changed at least once a day.

General Hygiene

As we were uncertain about the immunity that the puppies received from their first and only feed from the mother, we were probably paranoid about cleanliness. We kept all of the feeding utensils in a plastic bucket containing a bottle steriliser. Visitors to the puppy room were kept to a minimum. Everyone who was given access had to remove their shoes, wash their hands and have their external clothes sprayed with disinfectant. For the first three weeks we always used micro-touch disposable surgical gloves while handling and feeding the puppies. If we had been to a dog show or had been anywhere liable to canine infection, we changed all our clothing before visiting the puppy room.

Weight gain

The puppies were weighed daily to record their progress and to highlight any problems. It was an evenly-matched litter: all were born at a weight of thirteen ounces, and body weight doubled within seven days. They had achieved five times their original body weight after twenty-one days.

Weaning

We started weaning the puppies on the eighteenth day. Their first solid meal was Farex, and honey with milk. On the twentieth day they had their first meal of scraped meat. By the twenty-fifth day the entire litter was lapping, and at long last, we discarded the feeding bottles. The Whelpi formula was replaced by goat's milk for all but one feed. It was finally phased out on day fifty.

Worming

On veterinary advice, we didn't worm any of the puppies until they were either five pounds in body weight or were five weeks of age, whichever was reached first. In fact, the first worming tablets were given on the twenty-ninth day with a second dose ten days later.

Vaccinations

To ascertain the level of immunity that the litter had received from the mother, blood samples were taken from one of the puppies on the thirty-second day. A 2ml sample was taken from the jugular vein and sent to Glasgow University for analysis. Eight days later we learnt that no immunity had been passed on, and we were very thankful that we had been so fastidious with our cleanliness programme. The litter were all vaccinated immediately with live parvovirus vaccine. At nine weeks they had their second parvovirus, and their first distemper, hepatitis and leptospirosis injections. At twelve weeks they had their second inoculation for distemper, hepatitis and leptospirosis, and at sixteen weeks they had a third parvovirus injection.

Conclusion

To summarise, we kept the puppies warm, fed them at regular intervals, induced the puppies to relieve themselves after feeding, and observed a very strict code of hygiene. We lost much sleep keeping to the exacting timetable we set ourselves, but nothing was too much trouble – it was a labour of love. The litter suffered no adverse effects from the experience: they were happy and contented throughout the early weeks. They have now reached the veteran age range and have obtained successes in the show ring, although they have only being lightly shown. One has obtained a Junior Warrant, a Challenge Certificate and two Reserve Challenge Certificates and sired three Champions. Although he will never be a top winner, we are extremely proud of his achievements and immensely grateful that our bitch's memory has been preserved through our own breeding.

REGISTRATION BY THE KENNEL CLUB

The breeder is responsible for the registration of the litter with the Kennel Club. Since April 1989 all the puppies in a litter that the breeder wishes to register must be registered simultaneously by name on the official Form 1 (green). The application form must be signed by the registered owner of the dam (the breeder), and the registered owner of the sire. It is advisable to apply for registration of the puppies soon after the birth, as the registration process takes about twenty-eight days – longer if the Kennel Club reject your choice of names.

SELLING THE PUPPIES

Most if not all responsible breeders of Salukis will establish a waiting list of prospective purchasers before breeding a litter. The Saluki is not one of the breeds that can be sold easily. It takes a certain kind of person to understand their needs and requirements; they are not the easiest of dogs to keep, and it is irresponsible and short-sighted to sell to someone who may be unable to cope with the demands of the breed. Legal responsibility ends with the sale, but a breeder still has moral accountability to ensure that a puppy is placed in a suitable home, and they should be prepared to provide alternative accommodation if the first home proves unsatisfactory – even if this means looking after the dog yourself. Equally, it is your duty to make sure that any dog of your breeding is well-treated and well-cared for. We always insist upon a condition of sale that stipulates that our dogs live in the house with the family, rather than being kennelled outside. Recently that stipulation involved us in a legal tussle to establish our principles, incurring heavy legal expenses – but we won, and the dog in question was transferred to a more suitable home.

We also believe that it is not the responsibility of rescue clubs to resolve problems created by unscrupulous breeders. Their resources should be channelled towards looking after genuine cases of Salukis that have fallen on hard times. Remember, you made the decision to introduce a litter of Salukis to the world, and so it is your duty to ensure its well-being, even when it is out of your custody.

A fit Saluki is a happy Saluki.

Chapter Twelve

GENERAL HEALTH CARE

The Saluki is a slow-maturing breed and has a life expectancy of between twelve and fourteen years; some have reached the ripe old age of eighteen. Every dog owner wants a fit and healthy animal, but problems are bound to arise from time to time. However, you can significantly reduce the likelihood of your dog succumbing to illness. The first step is to get into the habit of checking your dog's skin, eyes, ears, mouth and anal areas during grooming sessions. Ensure that you worm your dog at least once a year, and keep up to date with the annual vaccination boosters. Obesity should be avoided; the Saluki should have at least the last two ribs visible beneath its skin. Hygiene is an important factor in health care, so make sure you keep your dog's eating utensils and bedding clean. Your dog will also need to be exercised on a daily basis. If you are observant and use your commonsense, you will be quick to detect any tell-tale signs that suggest your dog is not feeling one hundred per cent. Look out for any departure from normal behaviour. For example: does your dog welcome you as usual? Does it drink excessively? Has it gone off its food? Has it suddenly gained or lost weight? Are the eyes bright and alert or is there a discharge? Check its motions: are they too loose, or is it constipated? Does it have difficulty passing water? Is it reluctant to go for a walk? Dogs are creatures of habit, and any deviations from the norm should be regarded with suspicion.

A healthy dog will usually have a moist nose, but do not be misled by a dry nose. Some dogs will sleep curled up with their head between their hind legs, and the nose will dry out in the warmth. If you are unsure about your Saluki's health, take its temperature to see whether you should contact your vet. The normal temperature of the dog is 101.5F (38.6C,) with a range of 101-102.5F (38.3-39.1C). The technique for taking a dog's temperature is very simple. Use a stubby-bulb thermometer and:
1) Shake the mercury down to around 36C
2) Lubricate the thermometer with a little petroleum jelly or vaseline.
3) Raise the dog's tail and gently insert the thermometer about 2.5cm into the rectum and hold it still.
4) Wait 30 seconds, then remove the thermometer and take the reading.

GENERAL AILMENTS

The following list of ailments are a guide to some of the more common problems that a Saluki may suffer from. Remember, if you are in any doubt whatsoever, contact your vet immediately – he is the professional, and in times of trouble he is your best friend.

Anal glands
The anal glands are two scent glands situated on either side of the anus and should empty every time faeces are passed, depositing their contents as a scent marker. If they fail to empty and become too full they cause irritation, and if this is not relieved the glands can become infected and abscesses may form. Prompt attention is necessary. The task can be quite easily performed by yourself, but it is advisable to get your veterinarian to show you the procedure the first time the problem occurs.

To empty the glands, take a pad of cotton wool and holding it across the palm of one hand, raise the dog's tail with the other hand. Position the pad over the glands, then with the middle finger and thumb either side of the anus, squeeze gently inwards (towards the anus) and outwards. This should release the offending matter from the glands. If your dog is particularly prone to this complication, increase the fibre content of the diet, for example: bran, can help to solve the problem.

Constipation
The symtoms are obvious and the treatment is simple. Give the dog approximately one teaspoonful of liquid paraffin, and this will prove an effective laxative.

Daily exercise is necessary to ensure good health.

Coughs

Coughing is a common sign of many canine diseases. A harsh, dry cough similar to whooping cough indicates kennel cough, and you should consult your vet for treatment. Do not take your dog into the waiting room. Kennel cough is highly contagious and although it does not put adult dogs at risk, it can prove fatal to very young puppies, old dogs, or dogs that are in poor health.

Coughing can also be caused by smoke or dust irritation, an infection such as bronchitis or laryngitis, distemper, or it may be a sign of heart disease. Don't overlook the obvious, it could be that the dog has something lodged in its throat. If the cough is persistant, or the dog is showing other symptoms, consult your vet immediately. Proprietary cough medicines, such as Benylin, are useful for relieving mild coughs, or for making the dog more comfortable until it receives veterinary attention. The cough may not appear severe, but if it continues for more than a week the cause should be investigated.

Cysts (Interdigital)

Interdigital cysts are soft, painful swellings which form between the toes. The cause is thought to lie in the sweat glands of the foot. The cysts may contain grass seeds and they can become infected by bacteria. Usually the first indication of cysts is when you see your dog continually licking between his feet. The most effective treatment is a course of antibiotics prescribed by your vet.

Diarrhoea

Diarrhoea is most frequently caused by digestive problems, such as a sudden change of food, feeding liver in large quantities, too much milk, or over-feeding young puppies. The best course of action is to withhold food for twelve hours in order to rest the stomach, but allow access to fresh water. When you resume feeding, give the dog cooked eggs, or fish, with plain boiled rice, and only feed in small quantities. The patient can resume its regular diet within two to three days when the condition has been corrected. If diarrhoea persists, or the dog shows any other signs of illness, contact the vet straight away.

Ears

It is important to check your dog's ears regularly for any signs of infection. Early detection and treatment can help to prevent the infection spreading to the middle or inner ears. Do not make any attempt to treat ear problems with proprietary medicines; these may be inappropriate for the condition.

Eyes

A slight, clear discharge is normal, and this should be carefully removed with a damp cotton-wool pad once a day. Specks of dust or dirt caught on the eye or under the eyelid can be removed by using the corner of a hankerchief. Pronounced and persistant staining on the face from a watery discharge, can be caused by blocked tear ducts or in-growing eyelashes. It can also be caused by conjunctivitis. The Saluki is a sighthound, and therefore its eyes are very important: if you notice any disorders, do not delay – seek professional advice, and only use veterinary-prescribed preparations.

Heatstroke

The commonest cause of heat stroke is when dogs are left in cars in warm weather. This can also occur when the car is in motion if direct sunshine comes through the rear window of estate or hatchback cars. Prompt action is essential. The dog's body temperature must be lowered by any means possible. Ideally, you should hose the dog with cold water or administer ice packs. If this is not possible dunk the dog in a stream or any other available cold water source. Continue any of the above applications for ten to fifteen minutes, and this should reduce the body temperature sufficently. Allow the dog to rest in a cool, quiet place until it has recovered, and then take it to be checked over by a vet.

Hernia (Umbilical)

The most frequent hernia occurring in dogs is an umbilical hernia, which is seen as a protrusion on the navel. It is usually caused at birth by careless handling of the umbilical cord causing a rupture. Most hernias are quiet small and have no adverse effects on either dogs or bitches. If the bump is a large and unsightly, it can easily be dealt with by a veterinary surgeon.

Lameness

If a dog suddenly becomes lame, give it a thorough checkover to try to ascertain what is the problem. If it is holding its leg off the ground, the trouble is most likely to be in the foot. If it places its foot gently to the ground or drags its leg, then the injury is likely to be higher up. Check the foot for impaled thorns, stone chippings, or balls of tar. Examine the rest of the leg for any signs of injury, such as swelling or damage to skin, and try to pinpoint exactly where the dog is experiencing pain. A simple limp, caused by sprains, strains or bruises, can be easily dealt with. Give the dog half an aspirin, this will relieve mild pain and it also has some anti-inflammatory effects. Apply a cold compress and give your dog complete rest. Fractures and breaks must obviously be dealt with straight away by your vet.

Parasites

There are a number of creepy-crawlies that infest dogs; fleas, lice, ticks and harvest mites are the most commonly found:

Fleas: There are several species of fleas that affect dogs and are liable to be around all year long. Unfortunately, central heating and fitted carpets have created the ideal environment for their breeding and survival. If you don't catch a glimpse of them on your dog's body, you will soon know your dog is playing host if you see it scratch frequently and bite at its coat. The answer to the problem is to use a long-lasting insecticidal spray (such as Nuvan Top), making sure you follow the manufacturer's instructions. This is the only effective way of ensuring dog, and household, are free from fleas. We are worst afflicted during the summer evenings, when our dogs go hedgehog hunting. The hedgehog must be the fleas' best friend with exclusive squatter's rights – unhappily they often pass them on to our Salukis!

Lice: These are much less common than fleas. They spend their entire life on the host, attaching their tiny white eggs firmly to the dog's hair. An insecticidal spray used every ten to twelve days is an effective remedy.

Ticks: These are most often collected on country walks, and they are picked up from blades of grass and on heathland. The insect firmly embeds its head into the dog's skin and enjoys a plentiful supply of blood. When it has had its fill, it should drop off on its own accord. However, ticks can be removed by soaking them with a swab that has been dipped in ether or surgical spirit. This makes the tick loosen its hold on the skin so that its mouthparts and head can be removed intact. If the head is not removed, a local skin infection may result.

Poisons

All houses, gardens and garages contain certain substances which can be poisonous to dogs. Young puppies are particularly at risk when they are going through the chewing phase. Prevention is better than cure: so store any harmful substances well out of reach of your inquisitive Salukis. Signs of poisoning are: sudden violent vomiting and/or diarrhoea, fits, foaming at the mouth, a staggering gait, collapse and coma. All these symptoms will require urgent veterinary help. If you suspect the dog's illness has been caused by a particular substance, take the packet with you to the vet.

Pyometra

Pyometra is a type of uterine infection which usually occurs one to two months following a bitch's season, and it is probably brought about by a hormonal imbalance. A female with pyometra is often listless, has a temperature, drinks excessively and urinates frequently. In cases of pyometra, where the cervix is open, there is a thick, red-brown, abnormal smelling discharge from the vulva. If you suspect that your bitch is suffering from this condition, it is important to seek veterinary advice without delay. Some bitches can respond to medical treatment, but the removal of the uterus and ovaries may be needed to save the bitch's life.

Stings

Wasps and bees hold a fatal attraction for Salukis, who cannot resist trying to catch them. Unfortunately, if the dog is successful it is usually rewarded by getting stung. If the sting is visable, pull it out with tweezers, and apply a strong solution of bicarbonate of soda. Veterinary attention will be needed if the swelling is acute or if the sting is in the mouth or throat.

Tumours

Most dog owners have a fear of all tumours. Fortunately most growths (fatty lumps, cysts, warts) are benign, i.e. they remain at the site of origin. Malignant tumours, which are cancerous, are growths that invade surrounding tissue and travel via blood vessels to other body sites where they grow anew. As the dog gets older you should keep a watch for growths in the mouth and on the outside of the dog's body. With bitches it is wise to check the mammary glands regularly for any growths. If a tumour appears, it is best to discuss the condition with your vet. Removal of a small tumour is a relatively minor operation.

Vaccinations

A number of vaccines can be given, usually all together, to protect against distemper (hardpad), canine infectious hepatitis (a liver inflamation), leptospirosis (liver and kidney disease) and canine parvovirus. After the first complete course of injections, which should be started between eight and ten weeks of age, annual boosters should be given to maintain protection.

In most countries rabies is present and vaccination against it is essential to protect both the dog and the family. At the time of writing, rabies is not present in the United Kingdom, Australasia and parts of Scandinavia.

Vomiting

Dogs vomit easily and isolated incidents are to be expected and should not be the cause for any concern. Some dogs will vomit or regurgitate freshly eaten food, and eat it again. This is usually because they have bolted their meal when they have been competing for their share with other dogs. Bitches also will regurgitate their own partially digested food for their puppies when they reach weaning age.

Vomiting is part of the defence mechanism of the body, enabling the stomach to get rid of excesses of food, unsuitable or decayed matter, or irritant material before it passes further into the digestive system and causes harm. If your dog vomits once or twice, is a little bit "off colour", and has no abdominal pain or temperature, you can probably treat the problem at home. Starve the dog for twenty-four hours and, provided the vomiting stops, give a light, easily digested food, such as scrambled eggs. If this meal is kept down, the dog can be given chicken or fish mixed with boiled rice the following day. If all is well, the patient should be able to resume its normal diet on the third day. The dog should be allowed to drink very small amounts of cold water during this period, but do not allow it to drink its fill, as this will probably lead to further vomiting. Prolonged vomiting, especially if it contains blood, or is accompanied by diarrhoea requires immediate veterinary help.

Worms

Regular worming is crucial to protect your Saluki against internal parasites. Adult dogs should be wormed at least once every year – every six months if in close contact with children.

Worming tablets together with dosage instructions (the dose is proportional to the dog's weight), can be obtained from your local vet. Any evidence of worms in your dog's faeces is cause for immediate treatment, and all breeding bitches should be wormed prior to mating.

Wounds

Whether or not your dog needs to see a veterinarian after sustaining a wound, depends a lot on the type of injury. Minor lacerations can be cleaned with hydrogen peroxide; its foaming action tends to wash out any debris in the wound. Larger cuts, or punctures caused by bites usually need veterinarian treatment.

GIVING MEDICINES

At some time during your dog's life you will have to administer medicine prescribed by your vet. Do not be tempted to mix it into the dog's meal, it may be too ill to eat all its rations, or it may detect that the food has been tampered with and refuse to eat it. The only way to be sure your dog has swallowed the pill, tablet or capsule is to push it to the back of the throat and hold the mouth shut until you see the dog swallow it. We usually sandwich a pill between two small pieces of cheese and offer it as a titbit, watching carefully to ensure that the pill is not spat out. Powders can be mixed with butter, jam or honey, and this palatable paste can be smeared on the tongue.

Liquid medicines should be given one teaspoonful (5ml) at a time. Sit the dog down, hold the jaws closed with the head tilted back (nose up). Pull out the flap of the lip on one side of the mouth to form a funnel, and pour in the liquid. Release the head after the dog has swallowed. A syringe or eye dropper can be used instead of a spoon, and so, in effect, you are force-feeding the dog.

Eye medication is most easily applied into the conjunctival sac. Use your thumb or forefinger to roll the lower eyelid gently down and squeeze the ointment into the space exposed. The dog's head should be tilted slightly upward. Avoid touching the eye with the nozzle of the bottle or tube, as this can injure the eye. To administer ear drops, steady the head, lift the ear flap back, and aim the drop down the widest canal. Close ear flap and gently massage the ear.

The Saluki is normally a very healthy dog and apart from the odd minor ailment you should only see your vet for innoculations and subsequent boosters. We see our vet more on social occasions than on professional visits! However, do not under-estimate the importance of the vet: one day you may need his skills to save your dog's life. The last thing to do is to wait until you need a vet before looking for one.

Appendix I

USEFUL ADDRESSES

AUSTRALIA
Saluki Club of Victoria
Elizabeth Guthrie
President
PO Box 159
Berwick
Victoria 3806
Australia

FRANCE
Club FALAPA
Presidence et Siege Social
Robert Grimberg
6 rue d'Andilly
95580 Margency
France

GREAT BRITAIN
The Saluki or Gazelle Hound Club
Mrs J McLeish
Secretary
Grove House
4 Watton Road
Knebworth
Herts
England

The Northern Saluki Club
Mrs A Davies
38 Lund Avenue
Framwellgate Moor
Durham DH1 5BJ
England

SOUTH AFRICA
The Saluki Club of the Transvaal
Ron Kaser
7 Oak Crescent
Bramley View
JHB 2090
Rep of South Africa

SWEDEN
The Saluki Club of Sweden
Jonny Hedberg
Hoguddsvagen 32
18162 Lidingo, Sweden

UNITED STATES OF AMERICA
Baltimore Saluki Club
Lisa Kerger
21 Dunmore Road
Catonsville MD 21228

Central Arizona Saluki Association
Elaine Bertagnoli
10615 W Avenida Glenrosa
Phoenix AZ 85039

Chicagoland Saluki Club
Suzanne Martinez
6 Ashbury Ct
Bolingbrook IL 60439

Dallas/Fort Worth Saluki Club
Pat Stokes
3620 Roosevelt Dr
Arlington TX 76017

Empire Saluki Club
Celeste Frasher
59 Mill Stream Rd
Stamford CT06903

Galveston Bay Saluki Club
Lynn Green
2502 Briarbrook
Houston TX 77042

Garden State Saluki Club
Dianne McHugh
47 Falcon Dr
Budd Lake NJ 08805

Puget Sound Saluki Club
Sally Bell
14118-228th Snohomish
WA 98290

Saluki Club of America
Carole Adley
Site 11 RR1
Winfield BC
Canada VOH 2CO

Saluki Club of Greater San Francisco
Joseph Pendry
756 Buena Vista Dr
Watsonville CA 95076

Saluki Club of South Central Ohio
Cheryl Holman
2843 Albright Rd
Arcanum OH 45304

San Angeles Saluki Club
Tom Stoner
15762 Fellowship
Valinda CA 91741

Southeast Florida Saluki Club
Toby Perkins
8747 SW 52nd St
Cooper City FL 33328

Upper Chesapeake Bay Saluki Club
Janis Copenhaver
Rt 3 Box 60A
Reynoldsville
PA 15851

Willamette Valley Saluki Club
Elizabeth Crait
17333 SE Colina Vista Ave
Milwaukie OR 97267

Appendix II

SUGGESTED READING

BOOKS

Al-Marsuban, IBN. The Superiority of Dogs over those who wear Clothes. Aris Phillips 1977. Translated by G. R. Smith and M. A. S. Adbel Haleen.

American Saluki Association. Caravanserai of American Kennel Club Champions 1927-77 and Caravanserai of American Kennel Club Champions 1977-87. Sally Bell, 14121 228th SE, Snohomish, WA 98290, USA.

Birrell, Anne. The Saluki Book of Champions Supplement No 3 1986-90. Anne Birrell, Willards Hill, Etchingham, Sussex.

Brown, Curtis M. Dog Locomotion and Gait Analysis. Hoflin Publishing Ltd, 4401 Zephyr Street, Wheat Ridge, Colorado 80033-3299, USA.
Brown, William Robinson. The Horse of the Desert. Olms Presse, Hildesheim, New York, USA.

Day. J. Wentworth. <u>The Dog in Sport.</u> S. G. Harrap and Co, London, England.

Dickson, H. R. P. <u>The Arab of the Desert.</u> Allen and Unwin, London, England.

Elliott, Rachell Page. <u>The New Dogsteps.</u> Howell Book House Inc, 230 Park Avenue, New York, NK10169, USA.

Hutchinson, W. <u>Hutchinson's Dog Encylopedia Part 43,</u> London 1935.

Miller, Constance O. <u>Gazehounds: The Search for Truth.</u> Hoflin Publishing Ltd, 4401 Zephyr Street, Wheat Ridge, Colorado 80033-3299, USA.

Saluki Club of Victoria. <u>Salukis of Australia and New Zealand.</u> Elaine Verity, 9 Wattle Avenue, Ringwood, Victoria 3134, Australia.
Serjeant, R. B. and Bidwell, R. L. <u>Arabian Studies II.</u> C. Hurst and Company, England.

Swedish Saluki Club. <u>Saluki: Svenska Salukiringens Jubileumsbok.</u> Jonny Hedburg, Hoguddsvagen 32, S-181 62 Lidingo, Sweden.

Waters, Hope and David. <u>The Saluki in History, Art and Sport.</u>
Hoflin Publishing Ltd, 4401 Zephyr Street, Wheat Ridge, Colorado 80033-3299, USA. 1984 (second publishing – first published by: David and Charles (Publishers) Ltd, South Devon House Railway Station, Newton Abbot, Devon, England. 1969.

Waters, Hope and Birrell, Anne. <u>The Saluki Book of Champions   1923-1980 (including Supplement No 1) and The Saluki Book of Champions Supplement No 2 1981- 85.</u> Anne Birrell, Willards Hill, Etchingham, East Sussex.

Watkins, Vera H. <u>Saluki: Companion of Kings.</u> Trendells Ltd, Critchmere, Haselmere, Surrey, England. 1974.

MAGAZINES

<u>ASA Newsletter,</u> Sally Bell, Publications Chairman, 14118 228th SE, Snohomish, WA98290, USA.

<u>Kiosk.</u> Saluki Club of Greater San Francisco, Wendy and Brian Duggan, 744 River Street, Santa Cruz, CA95060, USA.

<u>Salukibladet,</u> B. Sudmark, Secretary, Forellvagen 4, 135 42 Tyresco, Sweden.

<u>Saluki Heritage.</u> Jeanna Jaques, Aldwick Grange, Boarshead, Crowborough, Sussex TN6 3HE, England.

<u>The Saluki.</u> Pamela Hargreaves, Editor, Little Standard Hill Farmhouse, Henbury, North Elham, near Canterbury, Kent CT4 6NJ, England.

<u>The Saluki Quarterly.</u> Published by Hoflin Publishing Ltd. 4401 Zephyr Street, Wheat Ridge, Colorado 80033-32990, USA.